Dream Catchers and Dolphins

Reaching Out
In a Time of Crisis

MARSHA FOREST
JACK PEARPOINT

INCLUSION PRESS

Canadian Cataloguing in Publication Data

Forest, Marsha, 1942–
Dream catchers and dolphins

Includes bibliographical references.
ISBN 1-895418-36-4

1. Forest, Marsha, 1942–   – Health.   2. Forest, Marsha, 1942–
Friends and associates.   3. Cancer – Patients – Ontario – Biography.
I. Pearpoint, Jack, 1945–   .   II. Title.

RC265.6.F67A3 1998   362.1'96994'0092   C98-932418-4

Published by
Inclusion Press
24 Thome Crescent
Toronto, Ontario M6H 2S5
Canada

Cover Design & Printing: New Concept, Toronto, Canada 1998

Contents

Dedication

To the Spirit of the Tuhoe

Treasures

friendship doesn't mean
proximity.
it is a bond.
closeness that flies over oceans,
flows through telephone lines,
is found in fax beams and electronic ether nets...

friendship is listening,
laughing,
sharing deep grief
deeper joy and magic...

friendship is a quiet trust
knowing inner circles are rare,
raw,
and few...

treasures.

Marsha Forest

Foreword

Paul G. Levy, M.D., FRCP (C)

This is a book about communication and mutual support. It is also a book about observing mutual support in action...and the growth that can come from that.

At one level it is about a person - actually, a couple - confronting a crisis in life. On the other hand, it is about a whole circle of friends - including caring, concerned people who might not have initially called themselves "friends," and including friends who live not just close by, but are dispersed across the face of the globe. And it is about this circle of friends all observing this crisis in the life of the couple; observing the efforts to cope with the crisis; in turn, many of them deepening their own ability to understand and cope; and then pitching in to contribute - through their contribution - to the healing process of coping and surviving.

In their e-mails, Marsha and Jack show a great deal of honesty and openness. They reveal their fears (about cancer, about death), their anger (about illness, about aspects of the medical system), their need for respect of their boundaries (to allow enough sacred space for themselves), their courage (in the face of illness and fear), and their determination (to carry on their life work despite daunting challenges).

Marsha and Jack arrive at new awareness, new insights - about life, challenges, work, death, community, support, love and prayer - and they share these insights with their e-mail community. It is clear that these messages inspire others. People are inspired to give support, to search within themselves on various issues, to be open and honest, to express their needs, to assert their boundaries, to meet their challenges, to carry on work that is challenging and difficult. Above all, people were inspired to be willing to connect with others, knowing that connecting - inter-relating and mutually supporting others - brings great satisfaction in life and accomplishes great things.

This book is about giving and being given back to. It is about sharing and having that sharing reap rich rewards.

There are other books that assess and discuss the power of mutual support. But this book, **Dream Catchers and Dolphins**, simply and beautifully shows us mutual support as it is happening - sometimes raw, often touching, certainly powerful, frequently poignant.

The unique medium that this network of support used was e-mail communication. It could have been smoke signals or Morse code. But this book is about how people used this newer medium, e-mail, to extend their support. It worked for them, and in this widely spread community, worked beautifully.

This book reveals the ways that this medium allowed mutual sharing and mutual growth among a wide circle of people. I know that the authors hope that the current readers of these e-mail letters will benefit too, the way their network did. Given what this book contains, I believe that this is inevitable.

Medical/Emotional Status Report
(Update just before publication in October, 1998)

Marsha continues to be well. Jack and Marsha are well and continuing to be each others' greatest supporters. They are writing and traveling and teaching and carrying their message to all who wish to hear it, and hearing back from all who desire to continue being a part of their circle. The network is in good health.

Paul G. Levy, M.D., FRCP (C)

Waves and Tides

David Hasbury

I stood on China Beach on the West Coast of Vancouver Island. It was a cool winter day, but the sun was shining through the clouds. I was all alone on the beach. The waves were gently hitting the shore, one after the other, a rhythm not unlike gentle breathing. I walked along the shore focusing on the beach, looking for stones that would catch my eye. All of the stones were wonderfully smooth, shaped and polished by the flow of water. Waves and tides had washed over them.

I spent most of the day there, listening to the waves, soaking up the sun, looking for stones, watching the ocean...and breathing. As the day wore on, in the distance to the south, a huge deep charcoal darkness was forming. The sky was slowly filling with cloud; the sun had less room to break through. Far off shore underneath the storm clouds I could see the shape of the waves changing. These same waves that were gently breathing on the shore were now rising, their caps were white, they were taller and bigger, yet the sounds of the shore in front of me remained the same.

The ocean is so large that I could watch all this forming before my eyes, yet it would be hours before the storm reached my shore. But I could see how all of the same ingredients,

water, wind, cloud, sun could change shape and the balance
shift. This scene became a wonderful metaphor for life.
Sometimes the storm catches us by surprise. Sometimes we can
anticipate its arrival. One thing is for certain — life will bring
storms.

When I began reading this collection of e-mail letters and
reflections, the metaphor returned to me. Marsha and Jack were
allowing those of us in their circle to watch and feel their
waves. Each message they sent came from a different moment
on their current journey through life as it presented to them.
Neither of them, nor any of us, wanted them to have to go
through the experiences that the visit of cancer would bring to
their lives. Clearly a storm was rising, but no one could see a
way of stopping it.

Instead they chose to share all that would surface through
this storm, with their friends. They simply chose to not be
alone in the storm, to gather comfort and wisdom from those
whom they love, and in so doing inspire and awaken us to what
is truly important in life.

Those of you who read these letters will have a strong sense
of lives rich with friendship, love, and wisdom. Marsha and
Jack do have a wealth of people with whom they share deep
and loving relationships. When the storm rose they were not
alone. Each wave that they experienced brought all kinds of
emotion — fear, hope, sadness, joy, anger, courage, and love.
Each time they shared with us, waves of emotion and strength
rose in response. Each wave carried new learning.

What is important to remember is that these relationships
which brought so much comfort and healing in the midst of the

storm, were born in much calmer times, when the waves were gently lapping on the shore. The richness we see and feel as we read these letters is available to each of us. Opening ourselves to those around us is a choice we can make every day. Being vulnerable is an option, and it seems to me that beauty is the experience that results when we allow ourselves to humbly be seen.

The letters found in this collection will definitely be relevant to those who have been "caught" by cancer. There is much that will be familiar, and this will bring comfort and inspiration. But this is not a book about cancer; this is a book about life. Cancer was the storm that blew into Marsha and Jack's lives, but there are no shortages of storm bringers to each of our lives: illness, death, divorce, violence, natural disaster ... the list could go on and on. We can survive life's storms, but if we share and learn through life's storms we can thrive. I know I'm working on this in the midst of my own storm.

Cancer's visit in Marsha and Jack's life has reawakened the knowledge that life is meant to be lived. This collection of letters reminds us that life is meant to be lived ... together. This book shows us how wonder, awe, wisdom, and beauty are multiplied when life is shared. It inspires us to live life more fully.

David Hasbury

Introduction
Derek Wilson

On Jack and Marsha's website (http://inclusion.com) there is a page that attempts to explain and give some context for Jack and Marsha's work. It's called, 'What Do We Do?' However, this title is something of a misnomer. What is on the webpage reads more like a 'What We Used To Do.' We learn that Marsha used to be a university professor, Jack used be the president of Frontier College in Toronto, and so on. Having set out to write this introduction, I now know why this webpage doesn't really deliver its title: there is no easy way to describe what it is that Jack and Marsha do. None of the usual rules apply. Jack and Marsha are not members of some bigger organization, they are not aiming to get rich, they are not managing a hierarchy of employees or handing out diplomas to trainees.

With Jack and Marsha what you see is what you get. There is no hidden agenda or covert selling going on. In this book, **Dream Catchers and Dolphins**, they tell it like it is. This is a 'live take' and there was no time for rehearsals; this is what they do. Over a two year period, **Dream Catchers and Dolphins** chronicles in searing detail the mountains and valleys of Marsha's struggle with 'cell disease' and the e-mail action of Jack and Marsha's wide circle of friends in support of this struggle.

But What Do They Do?

Jack and Marsha travel world-wide presenting, coaching, teaching, and connecting on the theme of INCLUSION and this work has enriched the lives of many people labeled disabled and inspired those that work to serve them. In **Dream Catchers and Dolphins** this life work comes full circle as Jack and Marsha tell how they faced the challenge (together with their circle of support) of practicing what they preach, coaching themselves and accepting the coaching of others. They succeeded.

There are no personal/professional barriers to hide behind here. For Jack and Marsha, their lives and their work are not two separate boxes, each with their own set of rules. Rather the roles of 'who we are' and 'what we do' are played in harmony, informed by the same set of values. This is why Jack and Marsha won't be 'retiring' any time soon and why **Dream Catchers and Dolphins** is such an important book.

This is a tale told in part through the thoughts and feelings of the circle of friends and the 'e-mail therapy' they offer. You will encounter an incredibly diverse range of characters in this chronicle. But what this diverse community shares is a commitment to inclusion. Indeed the dream of inclusion for all is what has brought this world wide group of people together, and in **Dream Catchers and Dolphins** they celebrate their connectedness through the medium of electronic mail. This is 'community' at the cutting edge, and sometimes that edge is raw, sometimes diamond sharp.

Who are the characters that make up this community? Again, there is no easy way to describe this cast of e-mail correspondents. Many have amazing tales of their own; some are finding their voices for the first time. What they have in common, although they have not all met each other, is that they are friends of Jack and Marsha's. This book can be read as an account of a circle of friends in action. They are a group of people mobilized by a crisis - Marsha's disease - and the individuals within the group are each striving to contribute to Marsha's well-being in the best ways they know. They appear on stage as themselves, not as the purveyors of 'professional advice.' Marsha is nobody's client in this book. They bring their own offerings of what is healing and their own memories of their past crises and pain, but mainly they bring their love for Marsha and Jack, and it is the many ways that this is expressed that makes this a tale worth telling, a journey worth revisiting.

To say it again, this book is not about something else; it is about what it is about. It is not a road map for some other journey. This is the road being traveled as it happens, blow by blow. There are no Ten Step Programs to Health contained within, nor any quick fix solutions to the problem of living. Jack and Marsha know all about the long haul, about how to endure, how to reconcile and rediscover forgotten values.

I would hate to be the person in the publishing industry who gets the job of categorizing **Dream Catchers and Dolphins** and indicating where in the bookstore it should be placed or what the subject headings on its back cover should be. There would be so many qualifiers: 'Relationships,' 'Health,' 'Community Studies,' 'Alternative Therapies,' 'Electronic Communications and the World Wide Internet Community,' 'Women's Studies,' and 'Disability Studies.' This is as it should be because Jack and Marsha are not members of any one department of knowledge or discipline. They are jackdaws of ideas. This means they are not proud or precious and are ever willing to notice, recognize, use and make their own, good ideas that grow up in any field of human effort. Matched to this, they are equally keen for others to make use of the powerful tools for change that they have developed, some of which are 'road tested' in this book. Indeed this is the reason for going ahead and publishing a book this personal and this painful: to share, and to let others know that there are other ways to be together and live and face crises.

Jack and Marsha have a keen nose for any ideas that are likely to lead to inclusive outcomes and that will get people to look afresh at what they do and why. It is often said these days that the sum of human knowledge is now too great for any one person to grasp, that there will be no more 'renaissance' men or women. This may be true for the world of factual knowledge, but it is not true for the world of ideas that matter. This latter remains a small domain and one whose content is the hardest to learn. This is the domain of knowledge where the key ideas will make sense to anyone who stops to listen, whatever their age or ability. There are no big words needed here nor tortuous chains of argument to follow. Everything can be said plainly, but it is often hard to hear. This is Jack and Marsha's domain and the subtext of **Dream Catchers and Dolphins**.

One periodical that won't be appearing in your university library anytime soon is the *'International Journal of Life, Friendship, and What Really Matters.'* If it were to exist, here is volume one, number one......

Derek Wilson
Nottingham, England

Marsha Forest & Jack Pearpoint

Why "Dream Catchers and Dolphins"

Why **"Dream Catchers and Dolphins"** as a title? Marsha writes:

While I was in the worst throes of anger, grief, pain, fear, etc., I also knew I had to be as positive as possible. I am generally a very positive person. But I was in the dregs of not feeling like a happy camper. I realized that allowing myself to feel awful was natural, cathartic, and good for me. At the same time, I needed positive images in my life.

Dream Catcher Image:
Among the Indians of the woodlands, the Ojibway believe that dreams have magical qualities: the ability to change or direct their path in life. Since the night air is filled with both good and bad dreams, one of the traditional beliefs was to hang a Dream Catcher on an infant's cradle board or in their lodges for the benefit of all. [They created the Dream Cathcers using loosely woven 'string' netting strung across a light-weight circular frame woven with bent twigs -- see the graphic throughout the book) When hung, the Dream Catcher captures the dreams as they float by. The good dreams, knowing the way, slip through the centre hole, drifting gently off the soft feather to the sleeper below. The bad dreams, not knowing the way, become entangled in the webbing, only to perish with the first light of the new dawn.

11

Dream Catchers and Dolphins

When I awoke each morning I saw the beautiful dream catcher given to us by John O'Brien. It hangs at the foot of our bed. Another dream catcher given to us by Trish Thomas from New Mexico hangs to our left. We are surrounded by Dream Catchers.

This serves as a metaphor, for in life we are surrounded by Dream Catchers, the people in our life who support us through thick and thin, reduce our suffering to whatever degree they can, and allow love and goodness to flow our way.

The dolphin is another story. When I knew I had to have massive and "aggressive" chemotherapy I also knew I had to design and create strategies to get through the process. I knew about imagery and had read enough about it to know I needed a personal and powerful image to get through the chemotherapy for six months. I had seen dolphins swimming in the wild in New Zealand. I loved watching their grace and freedom. This would be my image: Dolphins swimming freely and playfully in the wild.

I also chose the dolphin as the reward I would give myself after the course of chemotherapy. Our friend Anne Malatchi invited us to her apartment in Cozumel, Mexico, where we would scuba dive, and we would also swim with the dolphins. We booked that trip as our reward at the end of chemo.

The dolphin imagery that I developed for myself went further. I decided that my very own special pod of dolphins would swim around inside my body and would eat up all the cancer cells. Then, they would swim out of my body to some far away place where the toxic materials would be converted to organic waste that would make wild flowers grow. My dolphins would be "warriors for peace," as I myself want to be.

My warrior dolphins were not exclusively playful; they had other special abilities as well. They carried torpedoes to "shoot the hell" out of any cancer cells that wouldn't go placidly into the night.

When I actually swam with the dolphins after the chemo in February of 1997, they actually let me hold them, stroke them, and even swim while holding on to their lithe and beautiful bodies. What a ride! "I'm cured!" I shouted as I swam around and around. I am convinced the particular dolphin who allowed me to take this wonderful ride knew how much I needed her.

All in all, the actual dolphins and the imagery involving dolphins -- as well as the imagery of the Dream Catcher -- played an important role in my healing process. Hence **"Dream Catchers and Dolphins"** became the title and graphic images for this book.

How to Get the Most Out of This Book

Here's how we think you might get the most out of this book.

We don't want you to think we are "special" or "unique," different from you or you or you. Anyone can do what we did in their own way. We happen to have a large circle of friends, locally and internationally. You may have a big or small family, a local circle of contacts, or just a few people in your life. The number of people you have is not what's important.

What matters is that you have at least a few people who you feel you can reach out to.

Fate, luck, chance — all are words that are important here. It may be your karma that you and your loved ones are never ill, will never suffer loss or pain, and will always be happy. We believe all of us meet happiness, joy, pain, sorrow and loss in the course of living our lives. In different intensity, these things happen to all of us. How we deal with them is another issue entirely.

This little book is a glimpse of twenty plus years of nurturing the seeds of friendship and love with our network of friends and our chosen family around the world. We did not create our circle as preparation for this crisis, we built it as part of living a full life.

However, when a crisis came, we reached out. We had

reached out before with smaller issues, but this was a big one. We needed a bigger response, and we got it. At the time, we weren't even sure why we did it. With hindsight, we realize it was a pure survival mechanism for us.

There was a disease problem, but the medical profession alone could not do the complete job. They cannot do the 'work' of building personal relationships in our lives. Whether part of their job should/could be to encourage this more is the subject for another book or article. We think that no one should be released from a hospital without the appropriate medication and a "prescription" for love, or at least some direction as to how to get adequate support. That is not a small project, but it is necessary if we are to have a healthy population.

The medical profession has a crucial role to play in the role of helping to achieve full health for everyone, as they have demonstrated in our story. One mistake would be to rely on them to build the supports necessary for whole and real healing. This would be pure foolishness. The medical system is designed to cure a limited range of diseases. Health is much broader and requires each of us to be active in building our own healthy support system. Therefore, our recommendation is: **Build Your Own Circle of Support, and Begin This Process Now**.

The truth. Yes, it is at times a pain in the neck to make those daily phone calls, write those notes and e-mails, and do all the little things that create and sustain a social network. But if we don't, we are allowing the most powerful insurance in the world to lapse. We pay premiums on house and car insurance without hesitation. What about investing in REAL life insurance that can actually guarantee more for longer than any commercial policy. The prior cost for this 'unsurance' is investing time in other people now. The premiums involve time spent with people -- friends and family.

We work with many people who have children with challenging disabilities. The only constant we see is that families who have a support network, a team, a circle of friends (whatever you may want to call it) can survive. Not only do they survive, they often thrive. Why? Because they are not worried that if they die their children will be at the mercy of the social service system or strangers. They know their children will be surrounded and loved by "family." By family we mean either biological or chosen friends who play the role of real family. The have acknowledged their mortality, faced it, planned for it, and thus they can get on with living every day - rather than incessantly planning ways to avoid death - which is an excercise in futility.

Therefore, one purpose of our little book is simply to say: Please call your friends and loved ones. Share joy and sorrow. Share intimacy. Let people know you love them, and more than that, let them know you need their love.

We feel it is a tragedy that many biological family members have caused each other so much pain over the years, that they can't even touch each other. What is even sadder is that we don't then reach out and create another family – one of choice – where we can all touch, hug, and love one another, in times of joy as well as in times of sorrow. This can be accomplished. It is possible and it is positive. We hope you will start now.

Jack & Marsha

Chronology of Cancer Occurrences:

1988
- **June 13 – surgery: intraductal breast cancer – lumpectomy.**

1994
- May 2 – our dear friend Sheila Jupp is killed in a freak buggy/car accident in England
- June 16 – in Texas, doing a workshop – received test results - cancer detected – by phone
- **June 28 – another lumpectomy... pre-cancerous tumour removed.**

1995
- July 28 – Preliminary Diagnosis of Ovarian Cancer – more tests
- **Aug. 4 – ovarian cancer surgery**
- Aug. 9 – released from hospital for six weeks of rest
- Aug. 15 – first chemotherapy treatment
- Oct. 17 - 21 – Winnipeg workshops – first after surgery
- Nov. 1 - 4 – Creative Facilitator Course - Toronto
- Dec. 12 – final chemo treatment in the series
- Dec. 22 – Baker family from Australia arrives for their first "white Christmas"

1996
- Jan. 4 – Bakers leave
- Jan. 5 – We leave for New York, then Vancouver for two weeks of workshops
- Jan. 28 - Feb. 10 – Cozumel – scuba diving trip
- Mar. 25 - 30 – Yellowknife, NWT workshops
- May 15 - June 4 – workshops in UK
- June 16-18 – Pittsburgh, PA
- June 19 - 23 – Texas Institute

- June 26 - July 1– Yellowknife, NWT workshops
- July 4 - 10 – Toronto Summer Institute
- Aug. 18 - Sept. 6 – Yellowknife, NWT workshops
- Sept. 10 - 14 – Calgary workshops
- Sept. 24 - 28 – Nelson, BC workshop
- Oct. 30 - Nov. 2 – Creative Facilitator Course
- Full schedule continues until...

1997
- Jan. 9 – discovered new breast lump – opposite breast
- Jan. 10 - Feb. 2 – many tests, leading up to surgery
- **Feb. 3 – surgery**
- Feb. 20   depart for Anchorage, AK workshops
- Mar. 1 – continue on to Yellowknife, NWT – more workshops
- Mar. 14 – radiation scheduled - delayed by one week due to unidentifiable rash
- March 27 – Radiation begun and continued several times a week until April 25
- Apr. 12 - 15 – short break in radiation in order to do workshops in Connecticut
- Apr. 25 – final radiation treatment
- May 2 – depart for Scotland and England for one month of workshops
- July 5 – 11 – Toronto Summer Institute
- Life goes on... (and on, and on, we hope!)

This chronology is included to make the point that we managed to continue our rather busy work schedule among the various medical interventions. With the exception of one cancellation, we are able to carry on. We managed to deliver the vast majority of our appointments and deadlines with only occasional adjustments. This was part of OUR journey to health, i.e. carrying on felt healthy and health producing for us.

Cast of Characters

We thought it might be helpful to the reader if we provided a brief sketch of some of the key people who made contributions to this book. Some are obvious in that they have written letters which are included in this text. Others are people who are referred to in various letters. All of these people are dear friends.

A note: The people who are quoted in the book are those who happen to fit into an "e-mail edit." This means that they were corresponding with us by e-mail. We want to firmly note that some of our most powerful support came from friends who were physically close by, and who chose to just 'be there' in person, and did not happen to be writing us by e-mail. These include: Cathy Hollands (and all the Hollands), Rose & Dom Galati, Barbara Seed, Judith Snow, Victoria Pollock, Dave Hasbury, Rudy Ruttimann, Nathan Gilbert, Susan Young, Budd Hall, Darlene Clover, Tracy LeQuyere, Sheldon Schwitek, Yves Talbot, Gary Bunch. Their words are not recorded here, (not recorded in the e-mail). Similarly, people who phoned and wrote by hand; their words won't be found here either, though their role was tremendously important and appreciated. We apologize to them, for not having their valuable words in print here. By way of explanation, we did not 'plan' this crisis. When the mail mounded several inches high (in printouts), we realized something profound was happening. Many months after the immediate storm had passed, we looked at the pile. We couldn't face it. Then Duane appeared and offered to have a crack at the editing. When Duane began editing, I gave him the e-mail files - because they were easily accessible. He took them to Nepal. As the book emerged, we decided not to try to make it a total and complete accounting. It was a 'happening.' The e-mail outreach to and from our network of support was the innovative part of our story, the part that stands out from the many heart-warming experiences we have heard about involving people-supporting-people-in-crisis, and so that is the piece that is documented here.

Who's Who in the Cast:
(arranged in alphabetical order)

Shafik Asante: Shafik was one of our closest colleagues and friends from the various summer institutes at McGill University in Montreal and here in Toronto. Sadly, he is no longer with us. He was a remarkably skilled speaker and community organizer. Based in Philadelphia, he was the founder of **New African Voices** and the Village of **Kumbaya**. Shafik is the "star" of two of our videos: **Shafik's MAP** and **When Spider Web's Unite, Shafik in Action**. He authored a companion book, **When Spider Web's Unite**. Shafik was fighting his own cancers in parallel with Marsha, however his twenty-year battle was 'completed' on Sept. 5, 1997. His wisdom and friendship was appreciated then - and still is now via video and his writings.

> *Shafik was a man of many talents. He knew every word of the score to HAIR. He played the lead in another life on a different stage. We shared a fixation on 'colored pens', telephone gadgets, and rights for all. His capacity to confront constructively was legendary. That's why he got in our videos. He confronted us. "Your videos are all white!" "You're right. So you'll do the next one?" And that's how it happened.*

Gary Bunch: Gary is a professor of Special Education at York

University in Toronto. He has been a part of our lives for decades - at Frontier college and now. Gary is one of those quiet, invincible, immovable supports that is "just there." Gary has been beside us in several crises, and he is always quiet, solid, reliable. He is also a talented researcher, and several of his books are proudly titles in Inclusion Press. These include: **Don't Pass Me By**; **Kids, Disabilities and Regular Classrooms**; and **Inclusion - Recent Research**.

> *Gary comes over for coffee and we figure out what we can do with the world's problems in an hour. Gary was there with Marsha decades ago at York, and now, he is with us both - still unwavering in his commitment to principles. We don't always agree, but Gary is there for the long haul. He beats me in golf too.*

Rose and Dom Galati: Rose and Dom are teachers to die for. They love kids – theirs and everyone else's. Dom sings to his classes. Rose mothers everyone. And underneath the veneer, they have a pioneer spirit that will leave no stone unturned to create full lives for their children – and all children.

> *Rose and Dom are Maria and Felicia's parents. Dom gives me badly needed golf lessons. Rose feeds us – Italian of course. They make us homemade tomato sauce. Rose brought it to the hospital, fed us, and re-upholstered our couch. Rose and Dom believe that it is a sin to leave people hungry.*
>
> *Recently, we were shocked and saddened by the loss of their wonderful daughter Maria. Our hearts have gone out to them, as theirs have to us.*

Nathan Gilbert: Nathan is the Director of the Laidlaw

Foundation. He is a clear thinker, and after many years of grant applications, we became co-thinkers and friends. Nathan has the same worry genes as Marsha, so there is ample room for synchronicity. Nathan is a wonderful father who understands the meaning of unconditional support.

Nathan makes the best potato latkes this side of....

Budd Hall & Darlene Clover: Budd is the Chair of Adult Education at OISE (Universty of Toronto). We go way back. He was the Secretary-General of the International Council for Adult Education while I was at Frontier College. I sat on his management committee; he on my Board. Budd is a brilliant poet. We trust each other.

> *Budd and Darlene are movie buddies. She chooses, we go. We eat at their place. Budd has a great voice. Darlene inspires him with her passion for life. She will get her doctorate soon – at last.*

David Hasbury: Dave is a friend, poet, colleague and member of our extended family. His personal struggles as a survivor of sexual abuse have turned him into a gentle, sensitive and skilled facilitator and a great listener. He is also a co-author of **Action for Inclusion**.

> *Dave and his daughters are regulars in the kitchen. They just dried their camping gear on the back line. Our car has made many journeys with Dave's guidance. He is part of the team. He has just moved back into the neighborhood.*

Te Ripowai Higgins: Our Maori sister/friend from New Zealand is a professor of Maori studies at Victoria University in Wellington. She is an emergent Tuhoe elder-leader, who is engaged in the campaign to renew and rebuild the culture and language of the Maori people of New Zealand. She has been a part of our Toronto Institutes, and travels internationally in support of her people. She is a precious gift in our lives.

> *We met TeRipowai in Argentina at her first international conference in 1979. She told us we would come to visit. A decade later we did, and we were adopted. We were fed, sung to, driven, fed, and toured and fed again – through New Zealand – the Maori way. And then TeRipowai came to stay with us. And now all the nieces and nephews come. It's like that.*

Dave Hingsburger: Dave is a remarkable author and speaker. His personal crusade is to bring an end to the abuse of all people, and in particular, people with disabilities. Dave tours the world making stunning presentations. His press, **Diverse City Press**, publishes several of his books.

> *There is the public Dave – brilliant, witty, incisive, powerful. And then there is the other Dave, with Joe, and their dogs. They are a great couple. Quiet, gentle, almost meek – but very loving. Joe grows giant tomatoes.*

Cathy Hollands: Cathy is the General Manager of Inclusion Press - and our lives. She is brilliant at both those jobs - and with her other job - mother of five, mate of one. Daddy Dave and her children - Jonathan, Joel, Alex, Danielle, and Emma, are not only part of the Inclusion Press team, they too are part of our daily lives. Cathy's support (and her family) were a necessary condition for our survival. Nothing has changed since. They are our family.

> *Cathy is the 'chair' of the 'back porch' group where one*

has 'permission to say it all' and everyone knows that not a syllable leaves that porch. Venting is a necessary process. Its precondition is total trust. Cathy even trusts us with her children!

Kenn Jupp: Kenn is a colleague and friend, who we originally encountered during our work in England. Now, he is the co-founder of an innovative organization supporting people to have full lives in New Jersey (Neighbours). Kenn is also a talented writer, entrepreneur and humorist. His lectures invariably leave people chuckling and thinking good thoughts about possibilities.

When Marsha turned 50, we sent invitations to friends to drop in. Kenn and Sheila got one - in Manchester, England – and arrived! We were stunned. It was a good party. We flew to England to support Kenn when Sheila was killed. Years passed, and in a new life, we rode in a limousine to the wedding party for Kenn and Patti. A lot of water under that bridge.

Gerv Leyden: Gerv is a remarkable educator at the University of Nottingham. We have partnered with him to reach out to families in England, and make a difference for children. Gerv is also a brilliant musician, a master of all things Gershwin, and the creator of great audio tapes that renewed our spirits when they were low. Gerv writes the equivalent of Monty Python scripts for our e-mail updates.

Gerv collects hats. Not just any hats. Real hats. He also ran the New York Marathon dressed as Robin Hood.

Tracy LeQuyere: Tracy is a force, an entrepreneur, a creative wizzard. We met at Frontier College. Tracy was the co-founder of the Beat the Street Project, (an outstanding literacy initiative for street people in Toronto). Today, when not travelling, Tracy is in the 'water business'.

Tracy has a Harley Davidson. I'm jealous.

John O'Brien: John is one of our most intimate colleagues and friends in our 'vocation' of changing the world. John is the "Grand Exalted Pooh-Bah" of Inclusion Press (his listing on our masthead). He has been one of our most trusted friends and advisors with our lives and our press. He has been part of our Institute Teams from the beginning of our Summer Institutes 12 years ago. We create and do workshops together. John is, among other things, a brilliant speaker, story teller and workshop leader. He and his wife, Connie Lyle-O'Brien, have authored many books, articles, journals, and more importantly, have contributed leading ideas and leadership in the movement for equality for all internationally. We are the proud publishers (and sometimes co-authors) of works by John, including: **Action for Inclusion**, **PATH**, **Members of Each Other**, and **Celebrating the Ordinary**.

> *John has 'his room' and 'his chair' in our house. He is allowed on the Inclusion Press computer. You know that means he is trusted. We also are the keepers of the scepter of the Grand Exalted Pooh-Bah of Inclusion Press, so you know the trust is mutual. John cooks a mean chocolate chip cookie, on which topic he is a world class authority.*

Victoria Pollock: Victoria doesn't "do e-mail", but her role as guardian angel and 'walking buddy' were and are key in Marsha's daily routine to stay healthy. Victoria and her daughter Irene are part of the fabric of our lives.

*Victoria is Marsha's walking buddy. She is just 'there.'
She often arrives with sushi. She gave Marsha her
famous Polar Bear - one of the key comforts for
Marsha. This is the Bear that was gowned and attended
the 1995 surgery.*

Sheldon Schwitek: Sheldon has being 'doing' inclusion in
daily life for a long time. In 'real' life, he is a talented artist.
But as a co-owner in the Judith Snow household, he hangs out
at our place, and we are regulars at Garden Avenue.

*Sheldon is a man of many hair colours. If advice is
needed - or on how to fix most anything, call Sheldon.*

Barbara Seed: Barbara hails from New Concept – our printer
for Inclusion Press. But she has also been a good friend for
untold years. Barbara has a house key, and a letter that says she
can make any decisions required for Inclusion Press if we are
away. Do we trust her?

*Barbara and Jack have an arrangement. When he
needs to talk, she comes and they drink his Scotch. It
seems to work for them.*

Judith Snow: Judith is impossible to put into a few lines. Two
of our books tell pieces of our history with Judith over nearly
two decades. (**From Behind the Piano** and **What's Really
Worth Doing?**) She is a remarkable woman of enormous
intellect and talent. Her drive frightens people. Her commitment
to inclusion is non-negotiable. She is fearless and has ferocious
love for humanity and for us. We share that bond and our lives.

*A few years ago, when Judith was being flown back to
Toronto from San Francisco by air ambulance (Lear
jet), her life was in peril with pneumonia... but she*

managed to get the attendants to let her peek out the
window to see the stars. She did it by winking in Morse
code. And she remembered that the attendant was good
looking. This is a woman with spunk.

DuaneWebster: Duane is a medical doctor who lost most of
his eye sight, so he can't practice medicine formally. However,
his talents are wide ranging, and he shares them. That is how
this edited book came to be. Duane volunteered. Thanks
Duane.

Duane and Jack 'played' together at age 6, and then
were roommates at the University of Saskatchewan,
Saskatoon. Duane is a traveller and a photographer.

Neil Webster: Neil has been a friend since CUSO days when
he was organizing projects in Colombia. Then we worked
together at Frontier College in prison programs. Today, Neil is
Director of the Bail Project in Toronto – and continues to be
one of the world's best listeners.

Neil is my 'lunch group' partner. We eat and talk. It's
good and we have been doing it for a long time. Neil is
a Winnipeg Bluebomber fan. Say no more.

Uncle Whitu: Uncle Whitu is a spiritual leader for the Tuhoe
tribe of the Maoris in New Zealand. He is a wise man, with a
wicked sense of humor. We met Uncle Whitu travelling with
TeRipowai. He gives us a piece of wisdom every time we visit.
He also prayed for us – and we for him.

Susan Young: We have known Susan for two decades - as a
teacher, as the Director of the Imperial Oil Charitable Foundation,
and now as a friend. She has always been far sighted and

willing to 'invest' in risky ideas. Susan has been a positive force, pushing us ever forward, and in some roles, sending cheques to make it easier.

Susan shares our passion for scuba diving. Dive, dive, dive.

Marsha's Introduction

Both of us were mildly terrified to read Duane's edit of the possible book that was emerging. Cathy sent the draft manuscript to Scotland for us to read. While sitting in the sun at Bonkle, Marsha wrote the following piece.

May, 1998: The manuscript hasn't arrived yet and the thought of publishing it fills me with a mixture of many feelings.

First, fear.
What if it's good and it gets published and then I die? Too many of the books I myself have read about people struggling with illness have an epilogue saying how sad it was that the author died two days after publication. Will that happen to me? Superstition. I must give that feeling up. Face the fear and do it anyway.

Next feeling. Fear again.
What if I really like the book and it gets published and is a success? What then? Hmm. Fear of success!

Next feeling. Fear yet again.
Do I really want to read and remember all those awful fears I felt? Will the writing really help anyone? Is it good enough or is it just self-indulgent? Fear of appearing trite or foolish.

Fear and then excitement.
I haven't even seen the complete manuscript and I'm filled with fear. Also excitement. Maybe it will be good. Maybe it will help someone as so many books helped me. Maybe that's the role I'm supposed to play in all this: to share my story, to

share my pain, and most of all to share my fear and my never-ending hope.

Aha, this now starts to feel like the truth, as my eyes well up with tears. I believe that anyone facing a crisis faces intense fear and anxiety. We each need a way to figure out how to deal with these fears. I reached out as I often do through writing, never for a minute thinking that a book might emerge.

Duane, our friend and editor must have thought it was worthwhile if he spent so much time working with the mound of material we gave him. He could have chosen other things to do with his time. Is our journey truly of interest to others?

I edit other people's books, publish other people's words and now suddenly I am faced with publishing my own. And not words about work but words about the very soul of me, a soul that was shattered like glass in dealing not only with one cancer (breast) but a more scary event for me (ovarian cancer).

The breast cancer was in a sense familiar. I knew it better. I had survived it before. The first round of breast cancer was in 1988. Then, we had another lump in June, 1994, that was removed, but was found to be pre-cancerous. [That was welcome news, but we can assure you that you go through the full gambit of feelings both before and after those encounters.] Then the ovarian cancer hit (August, 1995) and then another new, separate and distinct breast cancer arose in January, 1997. It felt like too much. I was overwhelmed and terrified.

"I can't bear this," I thought. "I can't bear hurting Jack like this. I can't deal with cancer." But deal with it I did. And like all else in my life, I didn't do it alone. That's why this is not my story but "our" story. Marsha and Jack dealing with life together, and with the help of many dear and caring friends

Cancer has definitely not been the focus of my life, and that too is why I am afraid of doing this book. I don't want it to become the focus. But as I write this (sitting in the sunshine in Bonkle, Scotland), I realize that the book is not about cancer, but about life. Cancer is only one facet of my life.

I have always been in love with living. The cancer just accentuated this – made me an even more passionate enthusiast for life.

I have watched too many friends die in the past years (from a variety of causes, including cancer and tragic car accidents) to not be even more aware of the beauty and grace of living fully each and every day. Therefore, I have decided to drop the fear about dying as this book gets published, and instead reveal my secret wish that "Dream Catchers and Dolphins" become a big hit.

By this, I don't mean I need it to make the New York Times Bestseller List, but that it may help a few women and men who, like I was, may be cowering in bed searching for some wisdom and some meaning in the darkest hours.

I myself found solace and healing in several books written by people struggling with and surviving cancer, and indeed struggling with and surviving life. Cancer is simply one facet of my life that has helped shape who I am.

For me, the cancer came at a time in my life when I was reflecting more than before on the meaning of life, the meaning of change and on the more spiritual side of things. As I said to my dear friend John O'Brien, "Having a potentially life threatening disease does speed up the process of wisdom." It has definitely speeded up the process of acquiring wisdom. It has made me listen more carefully to myself and others, and though I am not of the "cancer is a gift" school of thought, it has definitely been a teacher to me on many levels.

To me, anything that happens in life is neither good nor bad per se, but is about what one makes of it. My only choice is how to deal with the hand I have been dealt.

I absolutely and resolutely refuse to be a victim or to play the role of victim. I realize I do not have control over much in this life, but what I can control, I will. What I can control is which people I wish to be closest to in my life, and what kind of life I will live, and how I react to the challenges that life presents to me.

And in this little book, dear reader, you will gradually see that it can take a whole army to keep one little human being surviving and thriving. I had a web of people and all their skills that allowed me to survive and thrive from the initial symptoms to the healing journey I now continue on.

I realized over time that my life is really no more vulnerable than anyone reading this book. I am now more aware of my mortality. Anyone of us can die in an instant but to live truly takes a lifetime. It is a learning I am happy to do one day at a time.

What did I learn in my encounter with cancer?

I learned that no one but me fully knew what my unique path to healing and to life needed to be. I now know that in each and every one of us is the answer to our own lives. I learned that I had to stay far away from people eager to give me advice and recipes for living. I chose to stay close to those who would listen, laugh and cry with me, and simply help me find my own road and path.

What worked for me may not work for you. Each of us can get ideas from one another and then choose what works for our own self.

Find your own path and follow it. If you change your mind next week, that's OK too.

And of course last but not least, surround yourself with love and with lovers of life. I prefer not to be around the "can't people." They kill my spirit and I choose to keep my distance from them.

I want to be immersed in life - the good, the bad and the ugly. The laughter, the tears, the sun, and the rain. For much of my life, I have tried to be too perfect, too achieving, too happy, too productive, etc. Now I want to, and I am learning to, make mistakes, misplace things, rest more, walk more, sleep more, and work less. I want to write more and read more. I want to be judged less, and I want to judge others less.

As I do this, I feel better and seem to make others feel better as well. I do not want to apologize even one little bit for who I am. I am who I am and I like me. I don't expect everyone to like me but I am delighted that several people who I love seem to love me in return.

When in crisis, do something.

Suggestion: Do what it takes for you to survive. For me, carrying on with my life and work was primary. I refused, and would not allow myself, to be treated like a victim or like a sick person. I saw myself as a "healthy" person who happened to get cancer.

Health, according to the literature I was reading, was defined not as an absence of disease, but as the ability to cope and deal with disease when it hit. For symbolic emphasis, I would not get undressed at the hospital until I absolutely had to. I wanted people to meet me and see me as a person first and not as a "patient". For this I was labeled a "difficult patient." So be it. Difficult patients last longer, so I'm told.

Suggestion: Build a team you trust. I would not see interns or residents without my primary physicians present. I was building relationships with my doctors. They knew me, my quirks and my personality. I knew them, their quirks and their personalities. I refused to see anyone but MY doctors. For this I was labeled a "difficult patient." So be it.

But I also brought little gifts to my doctors and nurses. I wrote them thank you notes. I saw the gradual process of them seeing me as a person and not as "the tumor in room 504". So they labeled me a difficult patient at first, but eventually a lovable person. And so, over time, I built a wonderful medical team that I trust implicitly.

Thank You and You and You – My Medical Teams…

Thanks are due to many. My key surgeon, Dr. Joan Murphy, was not only a brilliant and skillful practitioner, but had a patient ear when I was most frantic. She said a sentence I needed to hear and that I will never forget. I wrote it down everywhere. "This is not treatable. It is curable." Although I didn't believe her at the moment, I wanted to believe her with all my heart. Those words from my surgeon were a beacon in my darkest moments.

Thank you to my oncologist, Dr. Michael Crump, who is brutally clinical and honest. "What would you advise your wife if she had ovarian cancer?" I asked him on one of my early visits. "My wife doesn't have ovarian cancer," he firmly told me. Good answer, I thought. I respected him for being so forthright.

I incessantly asked him about survival, about guarantees. Never once did he capitulate to coddling me. He was honest. He said my chances of survival were good, but he wouldn't play my guarantees game. Because of this I trusted Michael completely. When I discovered he had three children, I brought 'kid stickers' for them. This has become a ritual on all my visits. I get great treatment; he gets great stickers for his kids. A good deal for us both in my view.

During my January 1997 regular checkup, a year after the ovarian surgery, Michael found a new and different little lump in my right nipple that everyone else admitted they would have written off as just another bump. Even some of the surgeons said it was amazing he found it. But he did. And because Jack and I followed up immediately, we caught another early, but more dangerous cancer. My new surgeon, Dr. Sidlovsky, a masterful breast surgeon, took out the lump and 18 nearby lymph nodes. He recommended radiation after the surgery. Back in 1988, it wasn't done routinely, but he explained that recent studies showed it was definitely a good thing to do. OK. Since I trusted these folks, I agreed. Thank you to Dr. Irving Koven and Dr. Sidlovsky for speedy and skillful care in the Mt. Sinai Marvelle Koffler Breast Center.

Dr. Koven and I go back a long way to the first breast lump and surgery in 1988. For years, I thought I had early "introductory" breast cancer. Then I found out I actually had a lumpectomy for intradual breast cancer –(found early through the intervention of my friend and family doctor, Dr. Yves Talbot also of Mt. Sinai Hospital). Yves thankfully set up an early mammogram in 1988, although I was not really scheduled for one. That early mammogram revealed the first tumor, which was subsequently removed. In 1994, Dr. Koven and I celebrated the 5-year tumor-free check-up. A year later, in 1995, the ovarian cancer trip began.

Now enters Dr. Anthony (Tony) Fyles and the medical team at Princess Margaret Hospital. New fears emerge. Princess Margaret is the new and amazing cancer flagship hospital in Toronto. But I somehow got it in my head that Princess Margaret and imminent death were linked hand in hand. Going there was doom. I was terrified.

This "doom and gloom" scenario was soon dispelled. My rational brain took over once again. The excellent treatment by Dr. Fyles and by his team, particularly nurse Noela Monagan, made me feel that Princess Margaret indeed was about life, not just death.

The team of nurses and doctors convinced me that I really had excellent chances for survival and that the radiation would increase those chances. In the surgical recovery period (before radiation began), we resumed our work schedule and did three weeks of workshops in Alaska and the North West Territories. Then, I did what was necessary to re-arrange my schedule so that I could be in Toronto for a month of radiation, and Tony and Noela went out of their way to make sure I could honour my work commitments. They made an exception and doubled some of the treatments so I could do a workshop in Connecticut (April, 1997) and so that I could leave for a work trip to Scotland and England (May, 1997). I see Tony every six months and also have total trust in him.

For me, keeping up our work schedule was not tiring, it was replenishing. For others, it might have been be exhausting to get on airplanes and meet deadlines. For me, going to the airport with Jack and feeling that plane take off meant life. I could feel my immune system go into action as happy endorphins floated through my system.

I weathered the radiation well and flew joyfully to England on May 2, 1997.

I want to express much thanks also to my family physician, Dr. Pauline Pariser, for her thorough checkups and warm personal care. It takes a whole village to raise a child and it takes a team of physicians to treat a serious illness. One is not enough.

Speaking of living, aside from the medical team above, two other doctors played a major role in my healing and recovery.

I do not put the Toronto General Team, the Princess Margaret Team, or the Mount Sinai Team in the 'friends' category. They are my physicians and good ones at that. From them I expect state-of-the-art care, caring, good service and skill. If they go beyond the call of duty, that is wonderful, but it is not essential. I think it is a mistake to want your surgeon to be a counselor, or to want your oncologist to act as a therapist. They can't. What they can be is qualified, up to date practitioners who act with respect and caring as physicians should. All of us, I believe, need additional support that is more and different than can be provided by 'excellence' in medical care.

I, however, needed more. I found it in two healers who have been indispensable. One is Dr. Shannon Dales, a young chiropractor, who was at my bedside at the hospital after surgery to adjust my body and get it moving as quickly as possible.

I needed Shannon for my body and for confidence building. She was there after surgery and before each chemo treatment aligning my spine, adjusting my body and giving me her youthful energy and confidence. She did not put me on faddish vitamin regimes. She studied what I needed and built up my immune system. She was always there when I needed her, and I see her regularly for adjustments.

But without a doubt, the most important single member of my medical team is Dr. Paul Levy. A psychiatrist in private practice, Paul was there for the healing of my wounded soul. Without Jack, I never would have survived. And so too, I believe I wouldn't be sitting here today without Paul. He is a psychiatrist who needs to be cloned. He is a healer, a mentor, and a friend. He has been there for me through thick and thin. He has definitely gone "above and beyond the call of duty," and he does this for other people he works with as well. I know, as several of my closest circle members see Dr. Paul as well. We refer to ourselves as "Paul's kids." He is there for us because he limits his practice and takes only the number of people he can truly "serve". Paul is a "servant leader" in the best sense of the word.

What makes Paul unique is that he has chosen to have a small private practice in a little, cozy, book-lined office that is a haven in this big city. He has no secretary and only a friendly answering machine to take messages. His office is the place where I shed my biggest tears and reveal my biggest fears. It is the place where I tell it all.

"Paul's place" has assisted greatly in keeping my wonderful marriage alive and thriving. Without Paul, there would be the danger of turning Jack into a therapist. Without Paul, there would have been the danger of overwhelming Jack with my fears while he was dealing with his own. Without Paul and a place to over and over and over again go through the fear and anxiety, I would have been hard to survive emotionally.

I don't care what anyone says, almost everyone faced with cancer, or with any other life-threatening events, is terrified. It is totally human to be scared. Not giving vent to those fears to someone, be it priest, minister, rabbi, therapist, husband or wife, etc., is dangerous to your health. Giving too much vent to your intimate partner on a daily basis can, however, take the intimacy out and put the caretaker role in.

I wanted Jack to remain my husband, and intimate partner. I wanted his intimacy and love in the middle of chemo or radiation. Jack and I were able to retain our intimacy as I found a different, safe and comforting place to put the screaming fears into perspective and to put the gushing tears into a well of healing.

Paul listened. And not only did he listen, he would take action. He would call my other doctors for information. He would feed me books and tapes. Overall, he would feed my soul.

Thank You, Thank You, Thank You...

This book is full of wonderful words from people all over the world. But also, I want to express special thanks to people nearby who didn't write e-mail and who were simply "there".

I can't mention everyone so thank you to all of you... you know who you are.

Thank you also to some who aren't here in the flesh but whose spirit lives in me. Pat Mackan, Sheila Jupp, Hardial, Raniera, Herb Lovett, Marte Woronko and of course to my inspiration Shafik Asante. He would have loved this book.

Besides all these letters, there also came an outpouring of gifts. Music tapes; meditation tapes; funny cards; T-shirts.

Thank you Pat and George for the gifts and cards. Thanks to all who sent music tapes, meditation tapes - and especially Gerv for the compilations of music.What did I do to deserve all this I wondered? Gradually, I learned to accept it and to just be thankful.

Marsha
July, 1998

Jack's thoughts
before reading the manuscript...

The truth is that I tried to edit these e-mails into something that might be useful some months ago. I opened the first file and had to stop. I couldn't read it. It was too painful, too close, too terrifying. I wasn't ready to 'relive' the experience, so I couldn't do it at all.

That was when Duane said, "I wouldn't mind doing a little editing." He was enroute to India, so we bundled up the e-mail disks and sent him off to contemplate the world and sort through the unthinkable confusion of e-mails – and see if there was something worth sharing with others. Months later, when we were working in Scotland (May, 1998), a bundle arrived. It was the draft manuscript. I looked at it, and did not even look past the cover. I knew I would need a block of time to read it. That happened back in Toronto weeks later. Marsha couldn't wait. She read straight through, and 'sorted herself' in a couple days. "Sorted" is a kind of Scottish expression that really fits the complexity of coming to terms with the manuscript – which she did. It took me longer.

When I read it the first time, I relived many hours that I have worked hard to forget. But I was renewed by the enormous energy and support that poured from soul to soul – via cyberspace. Occasionally I would find myself thinking that this is quite a story – only to discover that I was in it. That was the other discovery. I had thought of this as "Marsha's book" – even when there was no book. The phrase was etched, so I was stunned to discover that I was the author of much of the text. That was not a 'conscious' process. It was an 'outlet.' It never even occurred to me that I had written anything. That was a shock.

WE would not be here if all that support had not been given – so often without asking. Marsha was the "visible" patient, but one of our learnings was that disease or crisis is a family affair. I needed support too. Differently – but support. My appreciation is echoed to the 'teams' that gave life to our life in difficult times.

And to Duane. Duane Webster and I played together in Saskatchewan when we were 6. Later, Duane and I were roommates at university. We have been friends for many decades. When trying to think, "Who could do this?" Duane materialized. It is a labour of love. We appreciate the hard work he did. And as a doctor himself, Duane was part of the support team. He knows hardship and illness from both sides, which is why I believe he chose to invest himself in this project. (He lost most of his sight from glaucoma and a car accident.) We think this might help a few people. That's what this whole story is about. Thanks Duane. We couldn't do it alone; you made it a reality.

The Context

This crisis, like this book, was not part of our plan. And yet, when it struck, we knew that we had to reach out to our network of friends for support. E-mail has been the mechanism for us to maintain our 'virtual network' for some time. Thus, the e-mail correspondence that emerged was the logical outcome of our reaching out and asking for support.

How did this virtual network evolve? What is the context within which this book emerged? First things first. Who are Jack and Marsha?

We are human rights advocates. We have been engaged in a variety of 'jobs' and 'professions.' Most of us met while attempting to expand the boundaries of rights to all people.

Jack began his exploration after graduating from the Univ. of Saskatchewan in Saskatoon. He went to West Africa with CUSO (Canadian Peace Corps) - where he worked in Ghana and Nigeria for five years doing resettlement and post war reconstruction in the former Biafra. In 1975, he became the President of Frontier College, Canada's oldest national literacy organization. During his 15 year tenure, he took the College into new urban and social frontiers - adding inmates and people with disabilities to the spectrum of people obviously excluded from basic literacy and from job skills, and who therefore deserve assistance and opportunities. Jack and Marsha are authors, creators (of various modes of conceiving and of teaching concerning the human journey) and workshop leaders who travel the world to give people the tools they have developed - so that people can make their own plans, and yet learn to work interdependently.

After Jack left Frontier College, Jack and Marsha created another venture to expand their outreach to include not only Canada, but the world. They created the **Centre for Integrated Education and Community** (founded in 1989), and shortly afterward, **Inclusion Press**.

Marsha and Jack met while touring China in 1976. (Marsha was born and raised in New York City, came to Canada in the 60's as a protest against the Vietnam War. She stayed.) Marsha had begun her Canadian career a professor of Social Science and Education at Waterloo University and at York University. After a stint as the "visiting scholar" at the National Institute on Mental Retardation (now the Canadian Association for Community Living [CACL]), Marsha joined Frontier College. From there, the plan was evolved to help build a society that would 'welcome' everyone, using the concepts of basic skills and human rights. Marsha wrote several books while at CACL and at Frontier College. Since then, our team has been writing, editing, and producing books and videos to support the building of communities where everyone is welcome, where everyone's gifts are nurtured and utilized, and where people are learning to "get along".

Jack & Marsha, John O'Brien, and a lengthy list of collaborators have made the world their target. They travel extensively in North America, Europe, Australasia, and beyond, bringing tools for change and hope for the future. On these journeys, like-minded change agents have gathered and together have become a mutual support network. They are everywhere. And that is how this strange and fascinating collection of people came to be linked, and how they came to be joined in support of colleagues in need.

The collection of e-mail letters in this book came into focus because of the occurrence and re-occurrence of a disease. But this virtual network of support was/is there all the time. And the network is reciprocal. Sometimes we receive support, other times we provide it. This collection reveals only a small part of this web. The full portrait would tell raucous tales of great parties, gatherings, and celebrations. We have learned to appreciate each other often, with occasions large and small. The other part of the web is tensioned by all our struggles and crises. We have had many of these occasions too. They would begin the day our Centre was created – with Father Patrick Mackan. Pat died that day – Nov. 23, 1990. It would recall Sheila Jupp's tragic death in a buggy/car accident in May, 1994. Marthe Woronko, part of our life, and on our Centre Board; died from cancer in Dec. 1994. It would deal with Shafik Asante passing from this world on Sept. 5, 1997. Te Ripowai's son, Raniera and granddaughter were killed in a car accident in Nov. 27, 97. Herb Lovett was killed in a car accident in March 21, 1998. Rose Galati's daughter Maria died in her sleep at age 19, July 14, 1998. Our network has learned to support one another, on many occasions, in many situations. We also remember to celebrate.

Our learning is that all of us need to build networks of support, BEFORE the hard parts of life occur, thus help to get us through to the better parts. Hard parts are part of life. No one is exempt. Our choices are either to suffer alone when the crises occur (which is both dangerous and painful), or to build a circle of support now, celebrate the good days with those people, then help each other through the rough patches when they inevitably occur.

It is working for us. And our simple motivation in presenting this book is to give an example of invaluable, indeed incredible support through virtual reality (e-mail) in the hope that perhaps a person here or there might take some similar action, might build their circle, and hopefully live a fuller life. This is neither a prescription for a trouble free life, nor a guarantee of a cure. It is an invitation to anyone who can hear it, to begin a journey of healing (not curing) that leads to a more fulfilling life (in our experience). This is not a "tell you what to do" book. It is simply an invitation extended with the hope that it will help even one person to reach out.

We hope you enjoy **Dream Catchers and Dolphins**.

Jack & Marsha

Important reading note:

If you are familiar with e-mail (or mail of any kind), there is a 'lag' between when it is written, then sent, and finally received. Even though e-mail can speed up the process, there are still lags. We would send out a general note. People actually get it and read it at their convenience. And then, many of us wait for the 'right time' to reply to things. Thus, the ordering of the e-mails is at times confusing. It is more or less how they actually arrived. But the different authors may well be commenting on something they read some time ago. As long as you know, you can live with it. It's the way life works.

One more note:

This is not ALL the e-mails. We tended to sent our messages out to 150 plus people. Many people answered - some many times. There are thousands of e-mails. We couldn't possibly print them all. We also edited some of the most private ones because they were NOT general - they were unique and powerful personal conversations. Most of our e-mails are included here, but if there are references that seem to lead to suggest some missing piece, it may be that we chose to leave that piece out. We hope you will understand this.

Paraphrasing the Mohawk prayer:

"We have done the best we could. We beg your forgiveness in advance for any omissions and for any errors which we may have inadvertently committed. Forgive us. We did our best."

Reading Note:

We have adopted a graphic convention in presenting the e-mail correspondence. We hope it helps to sort which is which as you read through.

The **Dream Catcher Image** heads the pages with letters **from Jack & Marsha.**

The **Dolphin Image** heads the pages with letters TO **Jack & Marsha from the cyber network.**

Dolphin Ride

In crisis is opportunity, so the sages say,
and perhaps this crisis will teach me to play.
Teach me to laugh more, teach me to be,
totally, fully, marvelously me!

For peace of mind I yearn,
Not to compete, but simply to learn.
I want more tranquillity,
time for more writing.
Listening more. Much less fighting.

A friend's constant love started my healing.
I'd lost my spark; I'd lost that feeling.
But his unwavering belief that
eventually I'd be well
carried me through my private hell.

Then, in a flash just the other day
I knew again I had found my way.
Two dolphins pushed against my feet,
Soaring through water oh so sweet.
I was taken for a ride, oh so grand;
then out of the water,
he took my hand.

The dolphins gave joy back to me,
restored my hope,
and made me see.

A magic dolphin ride
turned the tide.

Embracing Uncertainty

There is one thing clear this summer night.
My fright which comes and goes
glows with a learning that envelopes me.

I am starting to see uncertainty
as creating a wise strong elder in me.

I saw two deer in a field today.
We stopped and looked at each other.
"Hello, please stay,"
I held out my hand.
They stopped.

I stood.
And for a magic moment
in a time which flew
I knew one thing was sure.
Nothing is certain.

A curtain of mist arose,
the deer froze,
I was kissed
by the warm summer mist.

The doe and fawn stood mute
in the light and
waltzed
quietly into the bush.

Walking home
I collected a bouquet
of what some call weeds.
To me they were flowering gems.
I cut the ragged stems
and presented my bouquet of flowers
to my friend,
a friend who sees me as I am.

I begin to embrace uncertainty.
There is no other choice.

Marsha Forest & Jack Pearpoint

Aug 02, 1995

Here We Go Again...Zap those Tumors...

(This was the first public e-mail from
Jack, so we decided to begin here)

There we were – "noodling" down the
Madawaska River last Thursday morning. This was a new sport
for us – floating on styrofoam tubes. It was glorious! And
likely still is, except that we aren't there.

In fact, we are a little tense. We do "hospital parade" every
day as we lead up to Marsha's surgery on Friday afternoon – a
radical hysterectomy. All this is to zap out a grapefruit size
ovarian tumor that remains the biggest painless misery we have
yet encountered. We don't know too much. And we won't until
after surgery – and then only a bit. The surgeons will report
back – but the biopsy stuff will take 7-10 days. It will be another long week.

The range of options goes from being totally benign thru to
the various stages of cancer. We have assembled quite an
impressive medical team (almost all women, including two
women surgeons) and they seem to have a general hunch that it
will be ovarian cancer – stage 1-2.

Marsha asked the surgeon, "Is it treatable?"
The surgeon answered, "No! It's curable. You are awfully
healthy – just not very well!" So that puts a positive spin on a
very annoying development.

Most important, it is a death threat and we've been there
before. It is not a death sentence. It isn't great – but life will go
on. Chemotherapy is probable – likely six treatments at 3 week

55

intervals. All this is conjecture – but the fact that they are even mentioning it sounds a great deal like preparation to me. So, at the moment, we need regular reminders to queue into the fact that life goes on. And we are going to continue to be in the middle of it...with a brief enforced rest period. We'll term it a "writing /editing break!"

Marsha has also decided that if she is going to have one operation, she may as well get everything done at once. So, she is also having a "*catastrophectomy*." This is cutting edge surgery – never before done. It is a unique surgical response to a terrible disease (common, but not unique to Jews). "*Catastrophizing*" is characterized by taking any situation and exploring all of the worst possible outcomes "in extremis" at high speed. There have been many drug therapies, but they tended to be so intense that addiction is a common side effect. So Marsha and Paul Levy have decided that the surgeon will, with a special flick of the knife, cut out the "catastrophizing gene" – and cure the disease. We anticipate minimal side effects, and a dramatic improvement in longevity. In fact, curing this ailment may add more years than the cancer could ever remove. So give us good vibes for **both** surgeries.

On the "lets be consistent" front, both Judith Snow and Cathy Hollands (Personal Assistant el-superbo) are having fits. They are both annoyed at Marsha. Each was convinced (inde-pendently) that they had the biggest, best, most painful, etc. ailment. Judith has grown a tumor too – also grapefruit size - but confirmed as a mere fibrous mass that causes discomfort. The debate has begun about shrinking vs. doing a "tummy tuck" (Judith's term). She was convinced this would earn major brownie points. Meanwhile, on holiday, Cathy cooked her kidneys and produced stones – ended up in hospital for two days – and is awaiting the next round of ultra-sound bashing. She is quite miserable and assumed that this would garner major sympathy and pampering. No such luck! Marsha, who is the healthiest of the lot, is whining louder than all combined since the hospital crew have removed "solids" from her diet. So she is constantly hungry – and endlessly letting all of us know. The hunger is actually a very good diversion from the other issue – fear. It's harder to make it go away.

Our Status:
We have cancelled our trip to UK at the beginning of Sept., since we know that Marsha will be "slowed" for at least six weeks. Other than that, we intend to proceed full speed ahead. Surgery is scheduled for Friday afternoon, Aug. 4. It will be 2-3 hours...depending on when they actually get underway. I will try to do an update soon after – when I get a chance.

As usual, in addition to the medical team, supporters are engaged around the world – from New Zealand and Australia, to the UK, USA and Canada. We will take all forms of good wishes, prayers, whatever – AND Marsha wants more "bookings". This is based on our experience with Shafik Abu-Tahir (20 years with cancer) who insists (like George Burns) that "he's booked".

And we have been listening to Kenn Jupp and hear the echoes of "No Dying Allowed". And the Elders and *whanau* of New Zealand send their support greetings directly thru the earth – bare feet to bare feet. So we have a lot going for us. And what we need from you is your commitment to keep us busy, as scheduled, and more. **More bookings is good.** It will force Marsha to get back on the road faster. Not too fast – but faster. Anyway, she just got new roller blades for her birthday (Aug. 10) and she needs to break in those wheels! My 50th birthday bash (still scheduled for Sept. 23) in Toronto will indeed be a celebration of life and love. Do drop in...

Marsha's "pre-op" imagery includes "Noodling down the river!", and a special act from *'Cirque du Soleil'* – wherein the two jugglers (her surgeons) work with the **All Star Act** (Marsha) and as they produce various luminescent balls, Marsha flings them into the universe where they are transformed into dancing stars. So if you want to "Image" along with us, you know where we'll be. Marsha says that I'm the "owner-operator" of the circus – keeping all the acts in line and the show on the road.

We want to hear and feel your **positive vibes** - and we wish each of you good health as we continue to struggle for justice for one and all, where human rights are not negotiable, and we are all included in healthy welcoming communities.

PS – My apologies for not trying to contact many of you personally and using this general notice instead. Under the circumstances, I didn't seem to have many alternatives.

From Marsha:
"Please send all wishes to BOTH of us, as together we are going to survive this and be even stronger and more committed than ever before (is that possible?) – to create a world where all are welcomed, loved and treasured for the gifts they bring.

Jack & Marsha

Dear Jack and Marsha

We are with you in the pain and grief, as well as sharing the hope and the optimism you have, as you start your journey towards the light. We are all in Gods hands, whatever that may mean to each one of us. And sometimes the best way forward is to return to the centre of life and wait quietly, drawing on the love and strength that lies there. Quietness and stillness create the room for healing, for both body and soul. Who knows which is in greater need?

Now I know this is Marsha we are talking about – which is like telling a space shuttle that its role in life is to stroll down the beach at sunset instead of soaring away into space on a great adventure. Sometimes having more means doing less. The gift of life has many faces, most of which are smiling.

Take this time to explore stillness and silence.

You are both in our prayers and thoughts

Love from John and Angie J.

Dream Catchers and Dolphins

 Jack and Marsha,

This actually should be to Marsha, but since you guys seem to be major league into sharing, I suppose it will be seen by her anyway.

Now about this tumour stuff . . . I think that tumours of whatever size, from pin point to football, are probably a serious issue and should be attended to with worldwide prayer, etc. However, it is very clear to me that Jack's e-mail is not a serious attempt to describe the catastrophectomy or whatever, but in reality, it is an attempt to throw some 44 people off the real serious crisis of turning 50. Having passed that mark myself, along with other deadbeats like Hitzing (whose response was, of course, to move to the retirement state of Florida), I can tell you that prayers are much more in order for those turning 50 than for those facing "ectomies" of whatever sort.

Now Marsha, as soon as this little thing is removed, you must begin to monitor Jack very closely. Anyone who can send 9000 units of e-mail, in an attempt to deny his own clear decline, is in serious trouble. Look for any of the following serious signs:

1. A growing desire to stay up late (defined as anything past 7:00 p.m. EST).

2. A compulsive interest in MAPS (now meaning those of the neighbourhood in metro Toronto) so that he can find his way to the street and equally important back again.

3. Long discussions of Snow, not of the Judith variety, but of the white variety. These conversations generally start in July and are accompanied by the wearing of heavy sweaters when the temperature plummets to anything below 27 C.

4. An interest in exotic foods – no longer meaning Indonesian, but now Puffed Rice with Honey, or creamed corn with low fat margarine.

5. Promises to begin the exercise routine tomorrow, and that means standing at least once every two hours.

6. And of course continued use of e-mail – to suggest that he is fine and that you are falling apart and blaming that on some perverse belief in Jewish doomsday beliefs.

So, I will actively and willingly participate in the worldwide prayer vigil for the successful removal of this "thing" and include the hope that it is indeed not malignant. I will also continue that activity assuming that chemo is needed. However, the heavy duty prayers will be for Jack and the hope that he can avoid many of the inevitable signs of decline now so apparent in my own life.

God bless.

Don   T.

Dream Catchers and Dolphins

Dear Marsha & Jack,

What a shocker! "Sorry" seems so impotent a word when discussing such a major event in one's life, but it will have to suffice!

Your email made me alternately cry and laugh. If that book on humour and medicine has any validity at all, I know that Marsha will come through with flying colours, thanks to Jack and all the good friends that surround her.

When my sister had cancer, I remember the nurses and doctors talking about a "fighting attitude" and how much a difference that makes in regards to one's recovery. They commented that, as a broad generalization, cancer patients tend to lie back and not fight, while AIDS patients tend to be fighters. Certainly I've seen exceptions and your attitude is definitely one of those exceptions! I know that it can't help but make your outcome more positive. Your attitude(s) is one that we all can, and should, learn from – in all aspects of our lives.

I laughed out loud at your "catastrophectomy." Being of the Jewish persuasion, I know I am very susceptible to that unique disease, and know many of my "ilk" who have succumbed. I am hopeful, that as yet, I have not had to deal with that – oh, I have a few minor lapses every once in a while, but I'm hopeful that I can escape the scourge of the disease!

I'm sure you've now been inundated with email (boy, some people will go to any extreme to get mail!) so I won't make this any lengthier.

Marsha, know that I'll be thinking of you on Friday. I don't know, I think it's not typical of Jews to say, "I'll be praying for you". I've always been somewhat uncomfortable with that. If people don't pray for you, are you bound for bad news???. Anyway, for me, I'll just say that you will definitely be in my thoughts. I know that with your strong mind and "damned if it'll get me" attitude, you'll do great!

Jack, I'll be thinking of you as well. I know this has to be so difficult – watching something you ultimately have no control over. But your strength will be felt by Marsha and by all those who love you both.

Your friend,
Barb   T.

Dream Catchers and Dolphins

 To dear dear Marsha

What's all this about more lumps? Where are they coming from? Have you been shoplifting again? I'm getting sick of lumps!!! Do you hear? Blind men will be touching you up – pretending to mistake you for Braille

Here are some reasons why things are not so bad as they feel:

(1) Had you thought that all this may just be a ploy by Jack to get you under a general anaesthetic so that he can get a word in edgeways at last!

(2) We could write a book about it afterwards. Call it "Make Friends With Your Lump." It has the ring of a best seller!

(3) Where do all these lumps go when they have removed them? Is it the same lump that is passed around and shared by everyone or is there a 'lump room' somewhere? Perhaps they keep it in the European Common Market along with the butter mountains and the wine lakes.

I love you Marsha, so keep on being you and DON'T DIE!!!!!!!!!!!!!!!!!!!!!

To Jack

Call me any time, any place, if there is anything that you need me to do. I will not be far away. I know how hard this is for you to be waiting around and not being able to DO anything. The power of friendship from so many people surround you both. Just call when you need to.

Big hugs to you both.

love Kenn J.

Dream Catchers and Dolphins

Dear Marsha,

Some things to remember today and tomorrow and Friday. You have a powerful, wise spirit. Your body has a great sense of timing – getting you to capable help early. You are on a journey of discovery and development that has affected many people – for the good. Your particular way of journeying comes from making the most of the lessons each moment. Part of your strength comes from the enthusiasm with which you declare the lessons of each stage of your journey. Whatever else cancer may be, it is a teacher for you, and through you, for many, many others ... including me, of course.

Your previous moments with cancer showed the importance of feeling your own strength, letting go of old self-hurtful ways, keeping clear of people and situations that are noxious, and drawing those of us who care closer to you. At moments you exclaimed about victory over cancer. Surely you have defeated cancer before, and it's important to recall that your body remembers how.

Now another test of spirit. Another attack in another (though related) place, and at an unexpected time. This teacher isn't finished with us yet. (If I had my way, the university of life would not have a required course in cancer at all; much less two.) The victories have been real, but the struggle goes on – and just when it's time to put *Inclusion News* together.

Part of your power comes from how vividly you experience things, how directly you express them, and how avidly you use your gift with words to extract their lessons. That makes the highs higher, and the lows lower, and the lessons clearer. It also can make me uncomfortable from time to time, because my emotional tempo is so much slower. This discomfort is, of course, one of the reasons I love you.

One of the things I admire about you is the courage you have in facing incomplete lessons. Unlike some of the dogmatists I could name (we'll get around to that in our upcoming paper), you are a fearless reviser in light of experience. This might be important now, because there might be temptations to question your strength: "It's back; maybe I was wrong, maybe I did something wrong." I am sure that the revisions in your lessons from this new struggle will be further purifications – refinements in the ore, in the furnace, making purer gold sense. (I think this worry about getting tripped by losing the ground under some of your understanding belongs to me more than to you, but I'll leave it here.)

Remember: "Together we're better" (Though you seem to be willing to go to excessive lengths to teach me this.)

Love,
John O.

Dream Catchers and Dolphins

 Marsha,

I called at an inopportune moment.... I won't bother you again tonight. I just called to let you know that the NW (moving SE tomorrow) edge of your perimeter of support is in tune with the effort. Will be doing my small best to align positive energies in your direction. I hope the great spirit has a sense of humour as I have not meditated enough in my life to get past the weird images of jello and chicken soup baths... I hope these distractions don't deflect the energy.

I am worried about the proposed catastrophectomy ... are you absolutely sure you have made all of the possible negative consequences of this as vivid as possible in your collective imagination?? What would have happened to Beethoven if he could hear well? You are a virtuoso catastrophiser and I don't think you should excise this gift lightly.

Will turn in for the post-op update; and I'll eat an extra portion of salmon at tonight's feast in memory of your fast.

Love and very strong and well founded hopes,

John O.

Dear Marsha and Jack

What can I say? Believe me when I tell you that I/we (Ken, Pam, Mark, Angela, and from work – Paul and Helen) are praying for you both. Since I collected your message, at 7.00am this morning, neither of you have been far from my thoughts – nor will you be over the coming hours, days, weeks. Dying is most definitely NOT PERMITTED! Each of you must take hold of life and each other and step forward. There is no looking back. There is no "maybe" or "if" or "but". There is only tomorrow. As I look to the future I see too much undone – too much yet to be started – too many people to help, for either of you to drop out now. Believe me when I say that I love you both and if it was possible for me to be at your side right now I would be. My God is with you both. As I drove home from work tonight I prayed in the spirit for you, Marsha, and although I can not be physically there God is with you. He is holding your hand. He is a presence at your side.

Marsha and Jack – may I add my image, my vision to your "All Star Act":
"I see an intense white light hovering over you both. It is the power of life, the power of promise, the power of good, the power of healing and wholeness; and MOST IMPORTANTLY – it is THE POWER OF LOVE"

God bless and keep you both.

All our love,
Ken, Pam, Angela and Mark.

Dream Catchers and Dolphins

Dear Marsha and Jack,

As my way of sending prayers and my love and support for you Marsha, and for you Jack (the circus manager), I am doing Tibetan overtone chanting. These will be done at several intervals, in advance of your surgery on Friday afternoon, so that the messages are sent to angels slightly ahead of the operations. A candle is being lit in a sacred place in our home by Christina and Jack; along with prayers for the successful elimination of all unwanted parts. A follow-up chant will be given over the weekend to help begin recovery. In addition, I will call up the drum spirit today (Thursday), and dedicate my drumming session this evening to you Marsha, and ask for spirit to do its good work across the ocean, with you and the people working with you, to remove the tumour and gene.

With love

Mark V. and family.

Marsha Forest & Jack Pearpoint

KI TE HOA PUMAU	TO MY BELOVED FRIEND
E to e te ra	The sun is setting
I te ra mere	this Friday
o Hereturikka	of August
ka haramaı roımata	Tears well up
te maringi me he rere	spilling as if a waterfall
te mohikuhiku nei	yearning
te whatumanawa	is the heart
te mamae o	for the pain
te hoa pmau tawhiti	of the distant friend
e huh ra	The thrashing
te hiku o te taniwha	tail of the monster
kaiapu o te tinana	consumer of the
	physical body
kei te aukume	tearing
kei te aukaha	gnashing
te tau a Whiro	is this disciple of
	Whiro (God of Evil)
take re te hoa	Rise up dear friend
i te to te riri	take the stance
	of battle
ano ko Tk-niwha	Just like Tk-niwha
	(The awesome God of War)

71

Dream Catchers and Dolphins

tona ito kia mate	His enemy to destroy
ko to patu	your weapon
ko to wairua	is your spirit
kia ara! kia matra!	Let it rise! be alert!
kia houa te rongo	Peace comes
o te pua po wananga	with the blooming of
	the white clematis
ko koe ra e te hoa	that is you beloved
	friend
kia noho tonu te kakara	so your perfume continues
ki te tauawhi	to caress
i te nui, i te paku	the great, the small
kia mau e te hoa	Remember dear friend
kei tawhiti nei	from here afar
te matemateone	is undying love
Na thoa pmau	From your dear friend
Te Ripowai	Te Ripowai

Heaps of prayers and love coming from all of us here – think of the noodling. I walked from the hospital to work – took an hour because I diverted for some bagels & lox. Found them –just thinking of you!!

Jack and Judith and the gang – hang in there – thinking of you too. Deep breaths!!!

TE

Marsha Forest & Jack Pearpoint

Dear Marsha and Jack

Surgery Tomorrow,
Some quiet verse for the two of you to share.

Love means......
that even without words,
we understand how each other feels.
Love comes quietly......
but you know when it is there
because, suddenly........
you are not alone any more
and there is no sadness
inside you.
Love is a happy feeling
that stays inside your heart
for the rest of your life.

Thinking of you constantly - Ken G.

Dream Catchers and Dolphins

 Hi Marsha and Jack!

Well, wow!

I want to be added to your circle, because ... been there, done that! I've had the grapefruit sized tumor (hysterectomy in 1991) and I'm here to tell the tale! I also know all the words to Hacoona Makata (sp.???). In fact, Dusty knows every word in both *Lion King* and *Beauty and the Beast,* and would be happy to re-enact anything you like at any time. (Remember, one of her dreams was to be on stage!) And I'm also into teddy bears. In fact, I'm wondering if Marsha would, at some point, be interested in a reading from *Winnie the Pooh*? None better.

My tumors turned out to be pre-cancerous, thank goodness, but the fear and surgery and &^%#@(%@*&^@!! were much the same. I also have had both breasts removed. But the point is that attitude is everything, and friends make it happen with you. And if you've got friends all across the world, all the better. So count me in!! And Jack, if you want a circle of husbands of wives who....., count Dale in!

Best of everything, you guys. I have not a tiny doubt that all will come out well.

Donna D.

Aug. 4, 1995

Still More Lessons to be Learned...
(after surgery)

I am sitting beside the bed. Marsha is gradually regaining consciousness. And she keeps saying, "Tell me the Truth!"

So, the truth! Although not yet out of the anaesthetic, Marsha's strength will pull her through, without further complications, and in flashes of clarity she waves greetings and acknowledges your support.

The surgeons, Dr. Wendy Wolfman and Dr. Joan Murphy, two rather extraordinary women with an equally extraordinary patient, reported that the surgery went well – technically. They found two ovarian tumours that were cancerous – the right larger than the left. They "appeared" to be early and isolated. There were no obvious related infections. They took extensive biopsy sections to confirm if there are any other problems. They are optimistic. It will take 8-10 days to get results. They immediately began to explore scheduling chemotherapy, and since Marsha is fundamentally so healthy, they may well begin chemo before they even release her from hospital. This is too early to tell, but the fact they would mention it is very encouraging. The "earlier" the cancer, the more aggressive the treatment – and that sounds pretty aggressive to me. The anticipated pattern will be 6 treatments – at three week intervals. Already the surgeons are suggesting that we should NOT cancel things – (although minor rescheduling may be required). Keeping busy is important to healing.

Dream Catchers and Dolphins

Temporary Hospital Information: Marsha is in Toronto General Hospital, Sixth Floor - Room 409. I don't think she'll be up for visitors or calls on Saturday - but after that...

We anticipate being home for her birthday – Aug. 10 – Thursday. If not, by then I think the medical staff may be willing to throw in the towel.

The surgeons were unable to comment on the surgical success of the *"catastrophectomy"* – and since many of you have questioned whether this is a good thing (I note you do it from afar), we will simply have to wait and see.

The "Together We're Better" contingent had many little adventures in the prep stage this past week. Firstly, Marsha needed a circle (as if she never had one before), but this was a "specialized" team, named the **Rose Quartz Team** – not Rose Schwartz as some have suggested. All members got their rocks...

Throughout the "pre-tests" this week, Judith Snow, Cathy Hollands, Rose Galati and Barbara Seed have been lurking everywhere – with "jello ovaries" (after the liquid diet was pronounced) and chicken broth al-la Calabria (Italy). Meanwhile, Te Ripowai has mustered her team – barefoot in the New Zealand winter – sending greetings – and threats – because another Mokopuna (grandchild) was announced – with Marsha and I as "grand parents" – and that *IS* a demand performance. Overtone chanting, drumming, candles, prayers of many denominations, prayer circles... around our house – our community and the world. We thank all of you because the first phase was to "get the tumours out." And that is done – in record time. Last Friday we learned they existed. This Friday –

they don't. Not bad!

Last night was enema night. This is worthy of a longer essay than I can record here. Sufficient to say that the wonderful theoretical concept about "home care" providing many services so you can do "same day admit," has a couple of systemic snags that have yet to be ironed out. All "came out" (as opposed to "turned out") well in the end; but if anyone had just said, "Do an enema," any one of us could have taken care of it. But as we all know, large complex systems are unable to answer simple questions without appropriate documentation and "official" sign off's at every level. So, the "game" of trying to find out:

1) when to do an enema?
2) were there any special requirements?
3) was any special equipment needed?
4) was someone coming?

The WHOLE Home Care bureaucracy was frazzled by about 7:30pm (24 hours after it was all guaranteed to be sorted) and just a few hours before surgery. At one level, all this is just slightly less than a cosmic joke – since enemas are not exactly high tech – and some of us have done them before – as did our grandmothers, and theirs before them.... BUT, NOT in the Home Care system! And it would have been hysterically funny – except that surgery gets canceled if the patient is not "preped". So we had a real problem – not just a joke. We were told it was a "special kind" of enema, and that "special equipment" was needed – and since we were not "special enough", a professional would come... And when they eventually did (after an emergency call – since the whole system collapsed, loosing both Marsha and her records), the person arrived with NO equipment – and a conviction that "the equipment" could not be found outside a warehouse, that did not open until the next day. Barbara and I went to a drug store and bought the "magical equipment" for $4.00 – in plastic – not stainless steel as was "required." But the good news is that it does and did the job!

Dave Hasbury and Susan MacDonald and Cathy Hollands and Barbara Seed and I sat on the back porch making inappropriate humour – while the procedure proceeded. Marsha was down to "shoo" everyone to their roosts while she settled in to watch *The Lion King*. She claims she also watched *Beauty and the Beast*. She did sleep the second half while "I kept watch."

This morning, Gary Bunch picked us up and we amassed at the hospital at 9:00. Rose Galati arrived with the beginnings of a "rose quartz douvet cover" – and then Judith, and Ian, and Barbara Seed, and Myrna Gilbert.....

The parade to the operating theatre was reminiscent of a dark ages execution – with Marsha leading the parade – singing. As we caroled several blocks of hallways, the attendant quietly nudged me... "is she always like this?" Another chorus of: "*Kummamutata*???", "*Whenever You're Afraid*", "*That's What Friends Are For*"... and on and on.

No theatrical agents responded with offers.. But teddy bear in hand, she was wisked into the inner chambers where humans may not enter.

Surgery was about noon – for 2 hours. Recovery room – 2 hours. Now she is here...sleeping – really sleeping – and I will shortly. Happily, because it is a long weekend, the hospital is empty – so there weren't enough security staff to even suggest to me that I must leave...

Gary Bunch's genes took a beating as we moved in on Marsha's room before she arrived. There were flowers – and paintings, and rose quartz, and oils, and wands, and a magic vest – and a beautiful quilt made by children – and dozens of little things that transform a room from institutional "sterility" to "I LIVE here!" Even for a short break it makes a difference. There are two teddy bears – her newest – Tony the Tiger (Esso) – who appeared from Susan and Tracy – and an older teddy that made it all the way to surgery – and came out with surgical gloves on to prove it.

I am now tired and rambling – but want all of you to know that we are disappointed on the one hand, but very optimistic. The doctor's line: "This is not treatable – it is curable". So once the anaesthetic clears, we will work on plan B – but it is a modification – not a change in direction. We may have to accommodate the high winds – but not often – and we are sailing on – full sail in a few weeks. Marsha may have a hammock on deck for part of the trip – that's about the only difference.

There will be additional news in 8-10 days when the biopsy results emerge – but for now, we are on the mend. Full full speed ahead!

Keep the cards, calls, and e-mails coming. Marsha and I both need it. And then don't forget, that Judith may need the same before the end of the month – for similar surgery – maybe. Have a safe and healthy day.

Jack - and a wave from Marsha

Dream Catchers and Dolphins

 Hi Marsha,

How wonderful to hear from you. We've all been so concerned about you and sending our good vibes hourly, so it was great to get a message from you with so much strength and humour in it.

As for your BSF test, we are in touch with the meteorology dept at regular intervals checking to see if any noises emanating from Toronto are exceeding 9.8 on the Richter Scale! So don't worry, I'm sure there's nothing that can't be put right by a strong curry and a generous helping of baked beans. (Sheila would have loved all this stuff. She and Jack would have had a ball with fart jokes!)

With big love
Kenn J.

PS – We'll come to Toronto when you've had time to recover. You'll know when. In any event, we'll be getting together in New Jersey next month.

In the meantime, Noooooooooooooooooooo dying!!!!!!!

Re: Still More Lessons to Be Learned...
Just to send my love, and this Native chant I thought you'd enjoy:

> I am a Circle
> I am healing you
>
> You are a Circle
> You are healing me
>
> Unite us
> Be One
>
> Unite us
> Be as One

love, Susannah J.

Aug. 6, 1995

Sunday update - Toronto General Hospital

The truth is we're both a little tired – and a little/lot scared. I have managed to stay in the hospital so far – which seems to make Marsha feel a little more "safe." Friday and Saturday were mostly post anaesthetic recovery. Poisoning your person into unconsciousness may be modern medicine – but fundamentally it remains a very crude club for dulling nerves.

Today, Sunday, Marsha is sleeping a lot – partially from exhaustion – and partially from fear. Now she is conscious enough to actually hear what the doctors have said. The phrases she has heard she repeats constantly: "This is not a death sentence!" and "This is not treatable, it is curable!"

All that sounds pretty good for a few seconds until we remember that the other half is "we have ovarian cancer!!" Marsha is not one to dwell on the negative, even for an instant, but last night and this morning we struggled with a spectrum of complicated emotions:

"Why me?"

"We already had cancer once!!"

"What if...???"

I refuse do dwell on "what if." Never seemed like a very productive use of time to me.. and after a few minutes, the Marsha we all know is back, preparing to give this cancer a one way ticket OUT. She has decided she doesn't want to kill all the little cells, but rather give them a guided tour OUT – where they can find a new occupation. Hopefully that job market is better than the Canadian labour market.

Today – Aug. 6, is the 50th anniversary of the Enola Gay dropping the bomb on Hiroshima. One article here stated that the world has spent $6 trillion dollars (1993 $) on nuclear research since 1945. That is $6,000,000,000,000,000!!!!! This is 15 times the amount estimated to eradicate world poverty.

Marsha will be starting Chemotherapy – likely next week. One of the drugs will be Taxol. It is relatively new – and very expensive. Good news – it just came under Medicare two weeks ago. Bad news – hair loss (temporary). Marsha is beginning to think about one of these new ultra short cuts in preparation. I am NOT. Mine seems to leave without any drugs from two spots already.

My wandering thought train – the great debate about "who should pay for taxol" – seems a deeply immoral question when we have already found $6 trillion for nuclear arms. Even if we spit it 50/50, poverty, health care, clean water – it would be possible for everyone – with a couple of trillion for special projects. And we certainly wouldn't have to wonder about "including" kids in schools and communities. Not that money is the block now – but at least that excuse would evaporate - and thus we could get on with the real issues about learning how to live together.

Recently we watched the BBC series (four hours) on the Crusades. It was brilliantly done – and ruthlessly brutal. That was 800 years ago. And today, as the troops increase the shelling in the former Yugoslavia (breaking the 'rules of war'– who dreamed up that oxymoron?), and as we recall Hiroshima,

Dream Catchers and Dolphins

I wonder – have we learned anything? Is our civilization any more civilized? We are here, by chance, getting the best medical service possible – and this week the debates in Ontario, across Canada and the United States rage about whether we should make the welfare bums work? Somehow from all this, we need to learn to listen deeper – to initiate different conversations. And part of me is very simple – I think that if ALL the little children began life together – and played in the puddles, and sang and flew kites together – perhaps some of these inter-generational insanities might diminish. I don't think they are born in our children – we teach them. So perhaps the work we do is really important – on the Anniversary of Hiroshima – so we NEVER do it again.

And that is why, after all the pain and anguish, Marsha and I will get better – be stronger – be clearer – do more. We may "do less" in order to do more. We have too much to do to quit just yet. And Marsha knows that.

I simply do not have the capacity to answer all your messages personally. I hope you don't mind. This is an endurance test – and I am assuming some communication is better than none. Keep your messages coming. We all need them. But we are both discovering that we need quiet time – alone and alone together – learning how to manage (if not control) the new partner in our life. This morning's prediction is that we will likely be released and return later – after the biopsy results – to begin chemo...

Jack & Marsha.
(Marsha is waving thank you for your notes...throat is still too raw for much talking.)

Visitors are welcome for SHORT visits. Phone calls are OK – but we are turning it off some times so Marsha can sleep. Our home phone collects messages - as does the fax.

We will likely be here till Wednesday? Thursday is Marsha's 53rd birthday so we would like to be home.

That's all for tonight folks. More later. It will be easier when MY computer returns to health (it died of sympathy pain on Friday morning – surgery morning). With the holiday week-end – I HOPE it will be functional on Tuesday. I have been staying at the hospital and only home for an hour a day so far. Cathy is covering as usual – but it will be easier when we are back home...

Thanks for all your amazing messages!
Jack

Dream Catchers and Dolphins

 *"Here comes the sun, little darlings*
Here comes the sun,
and I know,
It's all right.

Little darlings its been a long a lonesome winter,
Little darling its been like years since its been here,
Here comes the sun,
Here comes the sun,
And we know,
Its all right"

I can't send you a Picasso or describe a Starry Night via the E mail but as Bob Marley said, "music keeps us together". I'm not sure if that was before or after he sang "get up, stand up, don't give up the fight". In any event "let the sunshine, let the sunshine in, the sun shine in." Those lyrics had not popped out of my head for a long time, I am carried back to 1968, driving from Milwaukee to Chicago to catch the Broadway tour of Hair. Moments like now make me draw on such memories. Perhaps it is my escape from the absence of not knowing what to say; or not wanting to say all the cliches that such times are full of; or really not needing to say what is well known. But we find our own way of saying it anyway. So to you two, and the circles of love and life that surround you, I wish you "the dawn of the age of Aquarius". And then maybe the folks, you (Jack) remind us of, that are killing each other in Europe could also find "harmony and understanding."

Love to you all,
Ian P.

Dear Marsha,

Your courage and resilience are amazing. Being able to feel the fear (tied up in all of this mess) so soon, sounds like a sure sign that you know how much support you have. Seems to me, it's not fear that's lethal. It's getting frozen in denial. Follow yourself back and forth – between the joy at being alive, the resolve to stay with life, and the fear of how much there is to lose.

I am amused with my imaginations of what your hospital room must be like. Too bad Fred Wiseman couldn't make a movie of it...

Be well!
John O.

Dream Catchers and Dolphins

Dear Jack and Marsha,

HEALTH WARNING: If you hate the first bit skip onwards – it gets better. I was going to delete "the first bit" but thought I would like you to read it so you can know me as I am.

My heart is beating very fast as I write this. I have been away for a wedding and returned to find your messages. You taught me to be truthful (really truthful) so I'll tell you – I felt like smashing the screen when I saw everything you said! Thank you very much for writing. I am sure it is good to communicate and I love the e-mail for it. I'm still feeling very cross. But as I write, I feel a bit less so. Of course the reason I feel cross is quite disgusting. I am cross at Marsha for getting ill...especially when she is so healthy! I am also very cross because I love her and the thought of losing her is as hard and horrible to take – as it always has been and always will be. Every time I tell the truth my heart beats even faster...I'm so afraid this is totally inappropriate and you can't stand it – but I do believe you can so here's some more. Like you, I have known people struggling with cancer and, to me, struggling seems somehow inappropriate. Why can't we simply accept, accept, accept......I do so believe there are many levels of existence and this is just one. Why not accept what's happening? Yet somehow people do struggle with cancer and I struggle with them. It seems to be the way human beings are made. We must reach for the horizon, climb the peak, grow towards the light. We are curious, we are hopeful, we are learning, we are living in this particular way. So now I've cheered myself up a bit and pray I have not upset you. I always remember one of John O'Brien's stories about an abandoned boy and a cave and animals. And mostly the thing I remember about it is that the boy sang to himself and **felt** stronger and stronger as he did so, and he **became** stronger and stronger. So, as you proceed into chemotherapy there's music from all over the world accompanying you, as well as all the songs you especially love and all the songs I especially love. What a concert!

This is not so much a struggle with cancer, but more a total transformation of any rogue cells that may still be lurking. With any luck at all, these rogue cells have gone away with your womb (womb is useful for keeping things inside).

Thank you and take maximum care till we meet again. I'll write again soon if you would like that.

With love from Linda S.

Aug. 9, 1995

We're HOME! We're Really HOME! YES!!!

About 2:00 p.m. today (Wed. – Aug. 9) we came home. Its bloody wonderful (mixed but fitting imagery! Cathy's kids helped move us in. Marsha had her first shower and passed out in her first real sleep in days. I'm puttering, exhausted, but so glad to be home..

The medical report is simple: bodily systems are functioning normally – with discomfort – but normally. First "solid" food was a tiny bit of jello. We had a little more today – and now that all systems have demonstrated that they are working independently – we could GO HOME!!! They have been wonderful here – but we need to be home. We need to rest – and not be prodded. We need **not** to be on the phone for a little while. It all takes energy and in the "first things first" manual – the phone is NOT number one – Marsha is. And I need some rest too. So if we are quiet we are healing.

And once we are there, we need to be very focused for the next round – the Chemo (both physiologically – and psychologically). This whole new notion of having cancer (again) is a real head trip. The key is that we have to learn how to live with it – without it running our lives. It will set and re-set many priorities – but like a ship with a mission in a storm – we can trim the jib to the weather. We can tack – but our destination (our work – our mission) is unaltered. How fast we go may get adjusted...

We are preparing to "live life – not die it". I realize that

90

coming from Marsha, this may seem a little over the top. Imagine living life **MORE** than we have! But that is our mission – each and every day. We don't know how long we have, but this is **NOT** new. None of us know. So watch out... we're going to **LIVE** every day – even more. And we hope you do the same. We (each of us) can make that choice even with cutbacks.

So, our plan is to have a quiet 53rd birthday tomorrow and then begin the training regimen to get ready for chemo. We had our first "introduction" this morning, and although we understand that they had to do it (and they did it well), they scared us nearly to death. And then talked us back into breathing. So, it is really good to be home with that behind us in one sense.

We know it will be a long hard battle (likely 5-6 months by the time the drugs are fully out of our system), but we will do it. It was just another unwelcome shock. Clearly Marsha will be very tired. It could be that simple – or it could be much more complex. We just have to DO IT – get on with it – and live!

So, effective immediately, we are switching our energy. Some goes to healing and the rest to "fleshing out" the imagery that Marsha will use during the Chemo treatments. They will likely take several hours – and even "western" medicine recommends "visualization" and "relaxation". So we are creating a visualization tableau... A few of you will recognize bits of it. For others – you will have to fill in the blanks. A few of you have recognizable "roles" – but you are ALL there. This is a ginormous HEALING TEAM FESTIVAL... The purpose will be to overwhelm us with positive vibrations and imagery – so that whatever is going on in the "present" pales into unconsciousness.

The Healing Team Festival location – where else – New Zealand – in the Uruwera Forest – at our own Marsha/Tuhoe Festival. We are ALL there – all of you who have been sending wonderful messages of support. We are ALL, hundreds of us, on the Marae (we are crossing protocol lines here – but this is a visualization so we have decided its OK). Marsha and I are sleeping in the corner of Uncle Whitu's marae – Uncle Whitu is between us – just like he was at our first festival. And before the sun rises, before the morning mist wafts – Uncle Whitu stands and chants the prayers like he always has – for a thousand years. It creates a safe place – where only the truth can be told – and disharmony is not permitted.

The sun is up. Te Ripowai oversees. Noti cooks. Judith organizes. The day begins. WE all gather at the border of the marae. Then there is 'the call'. It is Te Ripowai, Rawinia, Aunty Uru, Judith, Barbara, Cathy, Rose... The call is the traditional Maori "welcome" echoing from the mountains, molded by the mist, swinging and chanting to each one of us – in a blanket of hope, hospitality and welcome.

Then WE all answer in song. This is a chant that feels as natural and necessary and as easy as our heartbeat. We are welcomed on the marae – and the day begins.

The "ringmasters" (sorry for the mixed metaphors – but this is Marsha's visualization), Te and Nick Marsh, announce the purpose of the day: to "sweep out" the cancer cells. Uncle Whitu says a prayer. Thomas lights a smudge and bathes us in the healing sweet grass perfume. And then: **"Let the Show Begin!"**

Rawinia, with the NEW *mokopuna* (grandchildren), is the team leader and calls the troupe to action. We are entranced, mesmerized, invigorated. We are a giant team. Pou Temara is our choral leader and coach. He had **all** of us up half the night for our dress rehearsal – and now it's "show time". The stage hands have given all of us our props... beautiful brooms – topped with rose quartz (thanks to Fran and Don). The brooms are more like wands – with balloons and ribbons galore. The working end is a special "Body Shop" creation of wonderful rainbow materials that will caress and collect "over-active" cells and give them a bath of "Forest Green Jelly" (this IS a Body Shop ad). Then it sends them off with creams and odours that will make them both harmless and welcome somewhere else, when they have learned to grow within the boundaries WITH all the other cells.

Act I: The "warrior defenders" (Marsha's friends – all of us) do a "*HAKA*" that would frighten the very gene structure of the cancer cells. Our message is that we are here to defend Marsha – and everyone else who needs it. We pound our chests, stamp our feet, extend our tongues and chant, hiss and snarl ferociously – to FRIGHTEN the cancer cells. The message is that we will fight – to the death – but you are welcome if you come in peace.

And then Rawinia signals to begin **Act II:** In our imagery the "challenge welcome" is accepted (although the fierce warrior stance is never far from the surface – in case it is needed). Our Healing Team creates an amazing new sound – a new chord – a healing welcoming sound that embraces us all. We all know the melody and the harmony. It resonates from us to the mountain slopes and back to Marsha – and all others who need support. And as the rhythm merges with our heart beat, we all begin the gentle sweeping celebration. It is not hard. It does not take stamina. Everyone does the best they can – TOGETHER. The cleaning/sweeping is gentle, complete, and spotless.

And then it is time to "pack up" and return to our homes until the next time. There will be six "healing festivals."

And Marsha and I, Te Ripowai and Judith will get on horses, or walk – or just materialize at Ohaua – a tiny magical marae high in the mountains. At this healing place, we will let the cool breezes and the healing mists do their work as the clouds fantasize a million new dreams. And when the wind has done its work, and we have picked the cloud with our dreams, we will return to continue our work.

And Uncle Whitu will ring the bell, and say a prayer and we will move on with his blessing.

And thus we welcome your participation in our healing visualization. Together we will be better. We need you – and you need us. It was always thus. So join us. Dates and times will come – but your participation will not be constrained by a western time piece. Send us your energy and we can share it around – we all need healing from time to time.
(Note: You are ALL included. Some of us have roles that are named – but we are all together on the marae....)

And as we sign off – from HOME – there was a wonderful irony today. We have been wonderfully supported by a superb medical team. The lead Surgeons were two wonderful women, and with them, a young Japanese Canadian – whose family was interned. Today, as we get ready to leave, is the anniversary of the bombing of Nagasaki. Strange how the world turns – and the children of people we bombed and imprisoned – are part of the team that is saving our life. So why do we have so much difficulty understanding that we really are in all this together. If we would spend a fraction of the time, money and energy learning how to live together – that we "invest" in creative killing of each other – what a world it would be. But we can do what we can do.... and that means living this day as if it is the only day of our lives. It is!

Have a great day.
Laugh, cry, let the mucus flow – but **LIVE** it – every day.

We are!

Jack & Marsha

Dream Catchers and Dolphins

 Welcome home!!

We have been reading all your & Judith's messages over the last week or so. Glad to hear you ALL (along with many people in the background who have been there with/for you) are getting through it all. Especially glad to hear about Marsha's bowels getting back to work!!

We have been thinking about you throughout the traumatic experience. I should think it was a whole new experience for the hospital staff involved in your treatment as well!

We realise you have more to get through yet with the chemotherapy, and are confident that you will get through it all with your fantastic attitude to life and all it can throw at you.

How could you possibly consider a catastrophectomy? This may well be at the forefront on medical technology/techniques, but please consider the final outcome: A NON-MARSHA TYPE PERSON. Can you imagine such a thing??!!?

Wishing you both a speedy return to full fitness and to your continuing love.

Kevin R.

Marsha Forest & Jack Pearpoint

To Marsha, my dream catcher, on your birthday

Roses are not always red
And I never thought violets looked blue
So here is my off-colour birthday wish
Especially written for you.

Your age demands a certain flair
To gain it you must now
Cut off your hair.
The chemo may help thin
That frizzy mane
But it'll grow back
And be curly again.
Don't distress if a few strands
Fall to the floor
You'll have that funky punk look
Which is never a bore.
Your new look will be sexy,
Daring and bold
And finally, perhaps,
You won't look soooo old (tee hee hee).

And when those drugs
Are zapping bad cells
You'll be in New Zealand
Listening to bells.
Your friends will be with you
And I, too, will be there
I'll be the one who is
Combing your hair.

Dream Catchers and Dolphins

Jack will bring water and
Food from the Gods
And Judith will bless it
To nurture our bods.
And we'll sing to the stars
And we'll dance in the rain
And we'll chant til our voices
Scare away all the pain.

So don't be afraid, pal,
We're in this together
The dream-catcher still holds
Our dreams on its feather.

So here is my birthday wish for you
(and I have no doubts it will come true):
You'll be a cranky,
104-year-old, long-haired Jew.

All our LOVE,

Jill, Bob, Rachel & Dylan

To the "Sweeping Team"

A Song for Our Labours

In many walks of life, it is good to sing as you labour. The rhythm keeps the spirit high, maintains the energy flow, and helps fellow workers coordinate their efforts for the efficiency and safety of all.

Marsha has requested that a large number of us be on her "sweeping" team - visualizing, along with her, a barrage of magical brooms cleaning the cancer cells from her body and returning them to the universe, where their life and energy can find more constructive expression.

So I thought I would compose a song to smooth and strengthen our labours. After much thought, and with Marsha's approval, I decided to use a Rogers and Hammerstein tune from *Oklahoma!* called, "Oh What a Beautiful Morning".

The visualization/singing day is Tuesday, August 15, and every third Tuesday thereafter for six times. Of course, time is a very fluid notion in the universe, particularly in the realm of visualization, dreaming and magic, so go ahead and visualize, sing and/or hum along whenever the spirit moves.

Having never composed anything more complex than a limerick before, this may take awhile. But here goes:

Dream Catchers and Dolphins

(Chorus)
I am sweeping away Marsha's cancer cells
As a magical maintenance engineer
On a cleaning crew stretching around the world,
With a vision that's shining and clear.

(First Verse)
We are sweeping with brooms made of pure light.
We are sweeping with brooms made of pure light.
Together we gently collect the debris.
The power of these cells we carefully free.

(Chorus)

(Second Verse)
Our team leaders sang up a fierce, chant.
Our team leaders sang up a fierce, chant.
We mean business, "You, Cells, you must get out now!
And become the strength that lets all of life grow!"

(Third Verse)
We sweep until Marsha is spotless.
We sweep until Marsha is spotless.
Together we clean up 'til she is pristine.
Then back to her work will go *Inclusion Queen*.

Love, Judith S.

Dear sister Marsha,

There are combined forces coming through and this is to further reassure you that YOU are constantly in OUR minds, sending the healing waves across the oceans. I have just this minute got off the tel to the uncs, and uncle Whitu says to remind you to remember what you both discussed the last time you had this. He is working full time on the prayer front – what with all his 'whanau' around the world in some sort of state of ill health or another!! You were on the priority list at their recent 12th prayer service at Waikaremoana. The 'blind one' said it was a huge turn out, including all of Ruatahuna and some from Ruatoki.

Noti is still here with us which has been a real godsend, with Danny recovering, and Rawinia still not quite 100%, and my visitors from South Africa. I've been telling them about PATHS, so you may be off there too soon. So *Inclusion Queen* (that's from Judith – I support that!), there's too much to do yet!!! This world needs you, like the rest of us!

I understand the mass email – you must do that, so don't feel you need to explain. I want you well – not spending unnecessary energy. Remember, I am 'receiving' between the lines. I – I feel and hear the silent secret personal messages. They come through loud and clear. I know when you are up and when you are down – and frighten. Do you know, I knew you would scream in the shower – I just knew somehow. Curled up with the bears on your bed scared and weeping silently, I feel those tears – I silently cry out, "It's OK Marsh!".

Dream Catchers and Dolphins

On my early morning walks (I do it more now so I can send you my energy) I sing, I cry out loudly, and I pray. I talk to you on these walks – so my day begins with all these emotions going, energising me to zap over in the ozone. I am not going to tell you not to do all of what is going on – you must let it out, the good and the bad. All you need to know is that there are many who love you even without the curly locks – that the lovely locks will be back even more bouncy than before!! There are those of us also who have absolutely positively undying *matemateaone* (love) for you.

Be scared and be brave when you go into chemo tomorrow!!

Just to remind you again to think of your special talk with uncle Whitu. He also asked after Jack and how he's coping. So I reassured him and like I've already stated before – ALL prayers are inclusive, as ALL are in some NEED!

I will catch up again tomorrow.

Heaps of love, hugs and kisses

Te

Greetings Gal Pal (and you too Jocko):

Hope you're feeling better (if slightly older) today and not too sore from the surgery. I've been thinking about you constantly. I know it's frightening, and there's little any of us can do but to acknowledge that, because it frightens us too.

Have you gotten any word on when you'll begin chemo, how often and for how long, etc.? I've been through chemo three times with friends and relations, and each of them responded differently...and you'll be happy to know not all of them lost their hair. Of course, cropped hair is all THE RAGE right now (the lead singer of the Cranberries looks like an ad for chemo). You've always been a bit on "the fringe", so now you might just look the part! Who knows, you might want to compliment it with a nose ring or a tattoo. Actually, I've been thinking, should chemo take a toll on your mane, I think it would only be appropriate for Jocko to shave his head as well...or maybe his beard...naw, his head, that way we could refer to the two of you as "our little cue balls" or some such nickname.

Well, enough about your hair. What I'm really concerned about is your head. How are you doing with all of this? Sometimes I worry that because you are so powerful and competent and independent and etc., etc., etc., you'll slip into playing that role, without even being aware of it, when all along we're standing here wanting you to lean on us. Do lean on us! Let us carry you as much as possible. This really sucks, you know. I just want to scream and shout and cuss and throw my fists against flesh; and I want to blame some God, somewhere, who wasn't paying attention and let this happen to you. And I try to be calm and intellectual and etc., etc., etc., but what I really am is angry. So tonight, let that be my way of supporting you. Tonight, while you're thinking good, healthy thoughts, while you're breathing deeply and helping your body to heal, while you're meditating and visioning your body free of cancer cells, let me be the one cussing and ranting and raving. Let it sap my energy, you need yours tonight.

All my love,
Jill   L.

Jack & Marsha,

So much power in believing...Tinker Bell really knew a good thing when she saw it!! You have an even greater audience, world-wide, that believes you can do it. We do believe!! And the applause is roaring, and the light begins to shine brighter.... I'm still on-line, even when my machine is off...

Love, Anne M

Dream Catchers and Dolphins

Marsha

Here you are, the one with this disease. Yet, there is this incredibly strong sympathy of souls because, when I read your thoughts and feelings (which run from chaos to calm), you so entirely express my own feelings, my own confusion. I, too, have times of optimism – broken by times of dread. In my head I think, "Okay, this is curable. She's gonna get the chemo and it will be tough but she will be fine and she will outlive me..."

And then I feel this panic creep over me and my hands start to sweat and my heart starts racing and I think about this disease taking even a small piece of you and the grief and anger become too much. Intellectually, I know this is survivable, but it's difficult to have confidence in intellect when I know you are scared and hurting.

You do need to prepare, physically and emotionally, for chemo. It may not bother you much, beyond a bit of upset stomach and feeling somewhat weak -- and that is what we're all hoping for. A lot of the side-effects, I've witnessed with chemo, take a harder toll on the partner than they do on the patient. You might experience mood swings, anxiety, etc., and Jack will be the one trying to respond. It's important that he has a lot of support. It sounds like your chemo cycle will be short, so I think it's very likely you won't have many of the nasty side effects, but if you do, there are some "alternative medicine" practices that are quite effective in reducing these .

I've been wondering if you went through chemo with your breast cancer? Medicine's understanding of chemo – why and how it works, how much is necessary, etc. – has come a long way just in the last few years. When my little pal, David, was undergoing three years of chemo for leukemia, they were constantly introducing new drugs, new protocol, better than the last.

Now, to change the subject. My poet pal/mentor, Albert Goldbarth, and I write back and forth a lot (via the post—he's anti-technology). His mother, who was quite old, recently died. Albert gave me this little description of her funeral, and given your shared ethnicity, I thought you might enjoy it, even in its morbidity.

So, here goes:

"Anyway, the funeral was followed by the ritual week of mourning – sitting shiva, as my Biblical people call it (I mean, of course, the ORIGINAL Bible, dearie). That meant smiling politely at about 8,963 people dropping by to pay their re-spects, with little monologues that generally went like this (only in a deeply Mel Brooksian Yiddish): `Oy, totteleh, could I tell YOU the stories! Izzy had a heart attack last year. A triple bypass. And then just last month, Pearl dropped dead from a heart attack too. Anyway, look, dollie, I brought you a food platter – chopped liver, lots of corned beef, and that good rich cream cheese you like so much. Eat, enjoy.'"

My advice to you, in terms of gaining strength and prepar-ing for chemo and life beyond, is the same advice given to Albert, in that thick Mel Brooksian Yiddish as he says: "Eat, enjoy." I'll write tomorrow.

All my love, Jill L.

Dream Catchers and Dolphins

Dearest Jack and Marsha

Wow! What an incredible co-incidence. Prepare yourselves for this. At exactly the same time as you have been going through your challenge, we have been too. It's a very long story, but to cut it short, John has just gone through (almost exactly) the same experience. Pain, biopsy, diagnosis, fear, etc. Now he is on chemotherapy – six courses three weeks apart.

Before this, he was fit and healthy. The rock behind the existence of so many people. Maybe too much of a rock because he held it all in and felt for others. Just like you guys feel for others.

He has lymphoma, with the equivalent of 8 apples in his stomach. But, spiritual healing is working well and the mass has shrunk tremendously. He had severe pain, not even controllable by morphine. With divine intervention, the pain went even before the chemotherapy. Doctors can't explain it, but we can!

You have all of the spiritual Aboriginal healing working on you now. Just feel it. Both of you are getting it.

We all need support. This has happened to two people who are best able to handle it – strong, caring, good, positive, with a great support network.

We were meant to meet, for this and other reasons.

We love you both.
Lyn and John – Bohdan, Yvette, Jara and the six animals

Marsha Forest & Jack Pearpoint

August 13, 1995

(Letter to John O'Brien)

Dear John.

E-mail is fine as a group but I need two or three private lines to a few friends who can hear me. Can you be one please? Can you cry with me on e-mail? Can I talk to you once in while? Will you maybe visit me? I am so scared, sad, mad, confused, dazed and shocked.

Now Jack is out for a walk. The sun is shining and I am crying my little heart out. What did I do? I was living and working so well. I don't understand this. I simply don't understand.

I must be strong and hopeful. They wouldn't do such intensive treatment if they weren't hopeful. It is too expensive. But the stage III (optimistic stage three) that they got out of me is no pretty diagnosis and I am terrified.

I don't want to lose my hair. Do you know anyone that has lost their hair and survived? Right now I'd like a few success stories.

I am rambling and before I go on much more I will wait and see if you agree to be one of my listeners. It may be hard but I need a few people besides Paul to cry and tell the truth to. You can write or call.

Tomorrow we get the chemo schedule. I am trying to stay

109

put – to heal from the operation which seems to be healing nicely.

Please in your way – help me make sense of all this. I am reading the *Tao of Winnie the Poo* and any mystery book available to me. Please, please be part of my team and help me. I can't do this alone. I really can't. I need your help. Jack is doing wonderfully, as we would expect. He is great and supportive and taking care of himself. I am trying not to drive him totally crazy. I get totally anxious when he's not around. I will learn to deal with that so I don't drive him away. This love stuff is so painful, but worth it of course. I couldn't heal without him.

Love. Marsha

August 13, 1995

Dear Marsha,

Of course I am here to listen to you. Anytime you like. About anything you want. I know that your great strength is entirely compatible with your falling to pieces from time to time and I am honored that you would like me to be a lstener.

Love,

John O'B

Dream Catchers and Dolphins

 Hi Marsha,

How wonderful to hear from you. I've just had a phone call from Mandy telling me that I'm going to be a grandfather! I'm not so sure that I'm responsible enough for that yet....old enough certainly, but not responsible enough.

Now, about this cancer! I have put together a list of advice and expectations you should have about hair loss, so sit up and pay attention.

(1) You should expect a hefty discount at the hairdressers...especially for perms and body waves.

(2) You should expect young children to stick their fingers in your ears and shout, "Dad, let's go bowling!"

(3) You can expect to win first prize in the spanish onion section of your local horticultural show...so accept nothing less.

(4) When you look in the mirror you can expect to look as if your shoulders are blowing bubblegum. This is quite normal for baldies.

(5) You should avoid taking unnecessary risks – like standing by pool tables, going to soccer matches and all ball games in general.

(6) You should expect to have to carry your dandruff around in your hands.

(7) You should not be alarmed by the occasional large chicken that decides to squat on your head and become broody.

(8) Expect Jack to use the top of your head to draw "MAPs", "PATHs" and other graphics ... but don't ask where he'll put the North star!

I love you megatons Marsha and am so very proud of you.

Big hugs

Kenn J.

Dream Catchers and Dolphins

August 19, 1995

Update from the Rose Quartz Warrior

On July 28th Jack and I began an odyssey of pain and fear that is now starting to turn into a journey of hope and healing. It is now August 19th. We are recovering from trauma, surgery, broken dreams, nightmares, and all the shit that goes with truly being alive.

We survived the first chemo treatment on Tues. Aug.15th and I am visualizing the chemo as being part of my first circle – an intimate companion to keep me alive. The first days after the treatment I felt I had been hit by a small red mack truck. But thanks to incredible new drugs the nausea was under control and I was just totaled. It could be much worse. Thank the goddess I am at home reading, resting and listening to music. Sitting upstairs and down, indoors and out, and learning to be humble in living with this process that will heal me.

The line I want everyone to memorize is the one said by my incredibly beautiful and talented young woman surgeon named Joan Murphy. "This is not treatable," she said. "It is curable!" That is our hope. That is all any of us can have each day.

I have in my head the beginnings of a small book. There is no way I would even be writing this without the love and constant support of Jack and also the incredible world wide network of love that surrounds us. Flowers, cards, books, videos, crystals, jokes, music all pour in from people every-where; and every note, every card, every line is a healing web as strong as the chemo.

I have friends who cook and friends who joke. Friends who laugh and friends who cry. Most of all there is Jack who is as hit by this as I. We will survive. There is no other choice. We will not just survive – we will thrive and go on to become even more humble and tender carers of life and living.

I need much solitude and quiet. I am a lightening rod for any negativity and am oversensitive to things that seem out of place. The small group around us respects our space and privacy and yet is there for us whenever we reach out.

My therapist and friend, Paul Levy, has been truly a godsend; as has a young chiropractor named Shannon Dales, who is keeping our central nervous systems in tact. The nurses and doctors at the hospital have been marvelous, so I can ask for no more on that front.

My taste buds are a bit wiped out and I am trying to eat and drink as much as I can. It is not easy. But life is not easy – that's for damn sure. But it is worth every minute!!

My polar teddy bear has accompanied me everywhere. They even gowned him for my operation. Every little bit of help is a comfort.

Ah yes, I cut my hair and it looks quite good. Rumour has it I will lose my hair, so I also got a cute wig. Covering all the bases as they say. I am taking it one day at a time.

Jack is going to do a workshop in Westchester at the end of August and I hope to do one or two events as the months unfold. We will take it one month at a time for awhile. We still plan to have Jack's 50th birthday bash and a team is forming to make it happen. It may be a bit quieter but it will happen. After all, how many times is a guy fifty? Send e-mail and faxes...

I am working daily on *Inclusion News* and editing a transcript of "SHAFIK'S MAP", our new video, which all of you must order (see I'm relentless). *Inclusion Press* is a real godsend and keeps my mind going. The real message in all this is – how can anyone survive without love in their life? Not me and not any one human soul.

I belong to an incredible network and I thank all of you, heart and soul, for being there. I am taking it slow and steady as I can't afford to get too up or down. Every day is something new and I need to stay strong and rested now in order for the treatments to work.

The only lesson here – **live and love** – **laugh and cry** and **let the mucous flow**. I hope this letter finds each of you living your lives beautifully and well and not creating problems where there are none. Thank you again for your love and support. I will stay in touch. Please forgive me if I don't answer every note personally. I am conserving energy for healing.

Much love from THE ROSE QUARTZ WARRIOR (known to insiders as the Rose Schwartz Brigade.)

Marsha Forest

Dec. 20, 1995

Saga of 95: Christmas/Passover Letter

Dear Friends,

We aren't going to attempt personal letters to everyone - but we do want to stay connected, so we have complied the **Saga of 95**. Another year in the life of Jack & Marsha.

We're nearing the end of 1995 - and very hopeful for a HEALTHY 1996. We intend to welcome it in with style - after all, it's the ONLY time we'll ever welcome 1996 - or any other year, day or hour - so we intend to enjoy them all. Marsha has finished the Chemo - and is beginning the detoxification phase. That means soon her food will not taste like platinum and other rarefied metal particles. By Christmas - turkey will taste like turkey. And we will be eating - with our Australian friends - the Bakers (5) and Judith and some of her friends, and who ever else needs a good meal that day. We're going to "do winter" and Christmas/Chanukah big this year as our Australian friends have NEVER seen snow. We intend to take them up the school house for a few days - where the solution to the Australian drought is piled 4 feet deep everywhere. We're going to do it all!

The Travel Half of the Year.
All in all, now that we are on the OTHER side of the cancer and it is in remission, we did have some great times in 95. The first half was packed with workshops - and finally we seemed to have the rhythm down so that they were getting better and better. We are finally learning to let go of control - and as we

117

do - people learn faster - deeper and better. It only took 50
years to figure that out. I am a slow learner.

We began the work year last year as we will this year - in
Vancouver. But last year, we went on to **Oregon**, where we
had a PATH workshop at the Flying M Ranch. It was as wonderful as the ranch was strange- and it was. From there we did
training events in Ontario and Bend, Oregon. **Toronto** was
next - where we were working to edit a new video on MAPS.
Remarkably, we were around when we were needed to support
my cousin Reg as his wife Ardath passed away from cancer.
From the funeral, we went to a week of training events - based
at McDonald's in **Chicago**. From there, a three day Conf. in
Denver. We ran errands and managed to get a NEW edition of
the **PATH book** out before plane time on **March 12- New
Zealand**.

Our southern trip was wonderful. We planned NOT to work
ALL the time - and actually began with a real holiday in NZ.
Previous visits had consisted of occasional days and weekends
slipped in between events. This time we drove north and just
wandered. We became "fisher people" with remarkable success. We fed a lot of people. We tried "deep sea" fishing, and
Jack is now a member of the "**Game Fish Tag & Release
Club**". A 360 pound, **7.5 foot Mako shark** nearly pulled him
out of the boat for 40 minutes before being photographed and
released for his lunch. **Scuba diving and snorkeling** were on
the list - and Poor Knights and the Rainbow Warrior were
visited - underwater. Jack continued his "flying" adventure as
a rank amateur pilot in several locations. We visited with good
friends, and with a little fishing, walking and general delight,
worked our way from the Northern tip to Wellington - at the
south end of the North Island. We did some excellent work
there and visited good friends. From there, we hiked one of the

great "hikes" in NZ - the **Tongariro Crossing**. It took a very long day. We climbed up OVER several volcanoes - some of which are active (and have since erupted). The day we chose it pelted rain all day - so we saw ONE kind of view. It is told that there are other views as well. We will do it again one day in the sun, but this was a great start.

The following week (Easter Week) was the **Tuhoe Festival**. We hiked to a magical place in the Urewera Forest - then down to the Festival location where we were consumed by Maori culture. The Maori "immersion" program was as exhausting as it was wonderful, it was time to move on to **Australia**. The Bakers (who arrive here Thursday picked us up and whisked us off to a rain forest retreat for the weekend. I **abseiled and we hiked** and ate - until recovered. The Work schedule resumed - full bore. **Workshops in Brisbane**, **Townsville** (with one day for a Reef dive) then **Cairns** and back to **Toowoomba, and Brisbane**. We finished our last workshop on May 4 - and dragged ourselves on to the plane home.

There was very little time to recover - do the mail and pretend to live in **Toronto** because we left for **Nottingham, UK** on May 24. We had one of our best ever workshops there with Gerv Leydon, who as a special treat took us on a personal tour of "Pierrepontte Holme" - my ancestral roots. The effigies had more personality than the residents by far. The **Bolton Institute** took the next few days - followed by two days in **Bristol**, an overnight in Toronto and a **week in Texas**. Our UK jet lag wasn't over, but we moved to **Richmond, Virginia** for a week of work. On that weekend, we borrowed Anne Malatchi's car and drove down the coast. We needed "space", so we both ended up **para-sailing** and **deep sea fishing**. We came back refreshed with a huge bucket of king mackerel. We had a day in **Philadelphia** with Shafik and Shina and company, then returned to Toronto on June 29, just in time to pick up **Te Ripowai** (from New Zealand) at the airport - her first North American. TeRip's spirits were excellent - but her body was very tired, so it was a special treat to be able to return some of her hospitality by nurturing her back to full health. A portion of her stay was spent at our **school house** - swimming, eating, walking and generally enjoying a quiet Ontario summer. We returned a healthy Te Rip to Toronto just before plane time on July 18.

1995 Part II

The holiday had been wonderful, so we returned to the school house to begin **the Inclusion News** marathon. Get that paper out. We started. While Te had been there, Marsha had noticed very light bleeding and phoned our Doctor. She said it should be checked, and booked an appointment in mid September. Meanwhile at the school house, we were asked to come to a meeting in Toronto. We decided to drive down - IF we could squeeze in a medical appointment at the same time. 48 hours tops. It was NOT to be. We got the appointment. We had our meeting, and since is was minor checkup - I went golfing and Marsha went to the doctor. At noon, July 28, I was summoned to the hospital. We met the doctor. She stated that Marsha had a tumor - **ovarian cancer**. Surgery was required immediately. One week later, Friday, Aug. 4 - bank holiday weekend - Marsha had successful major surgery - a radical hysterectomy.

On Aug. 9, Marsha came **home** - for her mini **birthday party on Aug. 10**. with a spectacular birthday cake on our back porch. It was a relatively quiet affair - but it was sooooo good to be out of the hospital that it was a marvelous celebration.

August was a bust of a month. I did a workshop in NY state at the end of the month - but it was a huge stretch at such a delicate time. Yves - one of our doctors prescribed "sailing" to blow out the rotten cells, so Marsha's first real "outing was Aug. 26 - sailing in lake Ontario. By Aug. 15, Marsha was strong enough from the surgery to start the **Chemo** treatments. It was roughly a treatment every third Tuesday - with Taxol and Cysplatinum being administered by IV for about 6 hours. The last treatment ended this week (Dec. 12).

I turned 50. The real date was Sept. 30, but Marsha would not allow such an occasion to pass by without an event. So, on Sept. 23 - over 90 people dropped by to eat, drink , sing, play music - and partake of a stunning prize Birthday cake created by the Hollands clan. The morning began with **50 penguins and flamingos** decorating the house, yard and block. It ended with song and great cheer - sentiments that we thought we had left behind.

The following week, Marsha broke new ground - and we traveled to **New Jersey** to do our first post-surgery workshop. It worked well. Marsha rediscovered that she could still work and the healing absorbed another surge of energy. We spent time with Kenn Jupp and Patti Scott - good friends and partners.

We worked "around" the Chemo schedule which slowed us down for one week after each treatment. Our next workshop was in **Winnipeg** - Oct. 17 week. From there we slipped into **Vancouver** for the weekend - **Mum's 80th birthday**. Sister Kate organized a spectacular brunch for about 35+. The cake said 50 + 80 - so Mum AND I celebrated.

We had a Chemo treatment on return - and were ready for our **Creative Facilitator Course in Toronto - Nov. 1-4**. This is our 4th annual. About 40 people came from all over the continent. It is our favorite course. One more travel event completed our fall season. We went to **Connecticut** - Nov. 11-16 where we did the third annual Creative Facilitator Course there - right on the Atlantic coast.

Although we were slowed substantially by four months of Chemo, being Toronto based, resulted in several unanticipated several positive outcomes. It helped us to **rediscover our home** in Toronto. After all the renovations of the past 2 years, it was wonderful to actually get to appreciate them - and we did. We also added. Moving back into the "office" meant it needed to be organized. Dave (Cathy's husband) is an architect. He offered to give a "little advice". We were shocked (and delighted) when architectural plans arrived for our **"airie" (eagle's nest office)**. Dave also supervised the contractor which unfortunately would require another 'book". The end result is stunning - with a great work space - and book shelves up to the skylights above our doors in the hallway - it is quite spectacular. So the **New office** was one great outcome.

A second outcome was our **new WEB Page**. I had been itching to get "on the net" for over a year, but I needed a block of time in Toronto, and it did not happen. But now, as Toronto residents, the opportunity emerged - so we leapt at it. So now we have the **Inclusion Press Home Page: http:// inclusion.com.** Altho far from complete, it is very exciting and we are already "linked" to other pages in England, Australia, New Zealand, Japan, as well as all over North America. Come and visit us on the WEB.

The third outcome was/is **Inclusion News** - our newspaper. Through all this, we have been editing and laying out the paper. It is now ready for press - at last. Copies for everyone in January.

December was scheduled to be quieter - in anticipation of the **Baker family's arrival** from Australia. We decided early on to avoid many events because Marsha's immune system was frazzled by the Chemo. Thus, **Judith** headed for San Francisco to attend the **TASH** conf. we were booked to attend. It was a good decision for us, but not for Judith. There was a terrible flu going around. Judith got it - and it turned into pneumonia. The good news, is that she flew back to Toronto on Dec. 4 - in a **Medivac Lear jet charter** - and is NOW home and doing fine.

However, she missed a remarkable day on Dec. 7 at **Frontier College**. John O'Leary (who succeeded me as President) and Budd Hall hosted a luncheon at the College to "unveil" the portrait of President Pearpoint - for their wall of notoriety. Thirty friends and colleagues roasted and paid tribute in a moving and much appreciated event. The timing was an extraordinary accident - six years to the day since we had flown from San Francisco to Asia - when we had to leave Canada to save our lives. The recollection was not easy - but it was important - and gave closure to a whole phase of our growth.

Now as we contemplate 1996, with all the cutbacks, and all the despair, we are enormously privileged. We have survived another death threat. In fact, as this year closes, we were able to reflect that these last six years, we have survived three death threats. Six years ago, we had to leave Frontier College - and Canada when a confused man was determined to kill me. In the incredible tension leading up to our departure, Marsha was diagnosed with breast cancer, had surgery, and five years later was one of those privileged to celebrate survival. That was brief, as a recurrent lump was removed (pre-cancerous), and we resumed our schedule. But this past summer, ovarian cancer gave us another reminder about our mortality. Having survived the surgery, the Chemo therapy and the trauma, it is our considered opinion that we don't need any more reminders. However, we have also had dramatic reminders that give one pause to reflect on the meaning of life - and for some, to "do what is important" and make dramatic changes. We have done that reflection, and we have concluded that we are living full lives. We are already doing what we love. We are making minor adjustments in our schedule. We will travel a little less and be more focused in our events - more "training trainers". We will take a few more "holidays". But, overall, it is a minor adjustment - fine tuning the balance - of a great life.

Five years ago, we decided to "build the press", and much to our surprise and amazement, we now have a very successful small press - **Inclusion Press**. We don't take any money from it - so it "looks" profitable, but the real success is that ALL our books have sold 5000 copies - and Action for Inclusion is now nearly 25,000. Our training videos are also going very well. PATH, MAPS and Circles have been adopted, or incorporated in provincial and state regulations all over North America, UK, NZ and Australia. And it works. So, we are feeling very good about what we do.

In 1996, we will explore the **Internet** - and perhaps make a CD-ROM. We have several books that will evolve - but no deadlines have been set. And if the mood strikes us, another video or two will emerge. In short, we are doing well.

We have cut down our travel plans a bit. We start in **Vancouver** in January. In March - we're trying a new location - **Yellowknife.** In **May - England. Texas - June**.

We want to be sure that we don't let moss collect where it shouldn't. So, we are planning some NEW ventures to "stretch" us - and keep us on the edge. The biggest risk - stretch will be the new **TORONTO Summer Institute on Leadership, Community and Diversity - July 6-13, 1996**. Some of the old McGill crew are gathering - but this will be smaller - more focused - and we are confident that it will work

- somehow. Although "affiliated" with OISE (U of T), it is our show - so there is substantial risk. But it will work...

And on the **holiday front** - we have TWO new trips planned this year. Firstly, we are going to Mexico, to **Cuzomel at the end of January** - for two weeks of Scuba Diving, deep sea fishing and archeology visiting. NO work. Then, in **November**, we are planning a major **Asian trip - to Tibet**. Duane Webster from Vancouver is doing the planning. That will be an adventure!

So, as we bring the year to a close, may we wish you a very merry holiday season: Happy Chanukah, Merry Christmas, Merry Kwanza, Happy New Year. May 1996 be peaceful, healthy and full of friends, daily delights and positive challenges.

Jack & Marsha.

Just a brief word from Marsha. Thank you all for the love and support from around the globe. What I learned is that without Jack's indomitable love, spirit and optimism, I couldn't have made it through these awesome months. Our work, our love and our friends got us through and we are better than ever - wiser, more focused and more humble.

May we wish you simply health, peace and love in 1996

Marsha

Dream Catchers and Dolphins

June 6, 1996

Welcoming June - Ten Months after Chemo...

Our "travel logs" have kept some of us in touch, but it seems time to update our progress in health and life, and thus provide an opportunity for re- and continuing connections with our "circles" of friends and family – our circle of life.

The summary is simple: Life has resumed! Some days somewhat more tentatively, but we are back up to speed. We are agreed that the "lessons" of Chemo therapy were quite unnecessary for us – psychologically – although they have definitely helped physiologically. We have always appreciated life – and continue to do so. We didn't need to be reminded.

The past two months have been a microcosm of our life for the past twenty years – yes twenty years! Twenty years ago we met – on a plane to China (May Day, 1976) – and so a new journey began. The beginning, the middle (where we hope we are now) and the future – have been "uneven," but never boring. We have been to some wondrous peaks – and we have slipped into valleys and swamps filled with snapping alligators. There are few regrets. We would exclude cancer if we could do it again – but as long as we can keep on going, we wouldn't have it any other way.

The end of April was like that. Marsha was (predictably) making all kinds of noises about "anniversary." We were busy doing workshops, and getting ready for the "spring tour." The residual chemo therapy effects were diminishing – so our daily "reminders" were shrinking to a "manageable" level. We are being very "intentional" about staying healthy so we can live the life we are choosing. Thus, Marsha included her annual mammogram in the week that we "did Nashville" after working in Kentucky. We got back on Monday April 22, but unfortunately, there was a "call back" from the cancer clinic – again. "Something" showed up. Mammograms induce trauma easily – and following shortly after ovarian cancer, anxiety was intense. (That IS an understatement!)

It was a long week.

On Thursday, after a four day "year," we had more mammogram "views." Good news – there was nothing! No breast cancer. The "good news" is that the newest radiography equipment is much more sensitive – so it shows much more detail. However, until they create a new "baseline," it results in many more "call backs" – the vast majority of which turn out to be "normal." However, the induced tension/energy resulting could melt polar caps, if focused. Hopefully the feedback "loop" that goes with the new equipment will build in faster feedback, fewer "call backs" and better "trauma management," as experience builds.

In keeping with our pattern (minutes after leaving the hospital) we drove to the airport, picked up Kenn Jupp and Patti Scott and had a wonderful weekend at our schoolhouse. We did a workshop in Bancroft on the Friday (April 25) and although we were tired – it was a wonderful and focusing diversion.

We had a final quick paddle in the freezing Madawaska

River, then returned on Sunday – in time to have a Board meeting of our Centre – at which we finalized the process of Marsha and I purchasing *Inclusion Press* from the Centre. We also had a mini "book launch" for the latest publication from our press – *Kids, Disabilities and Regular Classrooms*, by Gary Bunch. (Order your copies now – avoid disappointment.)

The following week was a "recovery week" – because we both discovered that this mammogram "reminder" was both unwelcome and exhausting. We needed time to get ready to "get on with life." As much as "nothing" showed up, the stress of the scare is intense – and it takes time, effort and rest to re-stabilize. In the middle of this, we are in the process of trying to "re-balance" Marsha's thyroid medication which not surprisingly was thrown totally out of balance by the Chemo. Trying to "interpret" which highs and lows are thyroid induced, and which are "pure stress," is a little confusing. So quiet time is an important piece in our healing profile.

And so, May day – the 20th anniversary of our meeting – was spent in Ottawa. We were part of a fascinating 3 day event at the Royal Ottawa Hospital – with child psychiatrists, social workers, teachers, families. David Schwartz, author of *Crossing the River* and a new friend, was the keynote. We will see him again. The truth is that conferences in "the belly of the monster" are very hard. In one sense, we did less (fewer hours of presentation), but because the energy is heavily weighted on the drain side (sucked out of you), we were more exhausted than from doing a full week workshop where we "work harder." But it is a shared growing. In those events, we give AND we are renewed. There was very little "renewal" energy in this conference. Judith was there and did an amazing job --

as she often does.

From Ottawa, we repacked our bags in Toronto and flew to Vancouver for the week. We did the keynote and a workshop for an International Deaf-Blind conference, (2 days). We had a wonderful one day planning/team building session with HOMES - a new "human service agency" in Abbotsford that is rescuing people from the Woodlands Institution, where they have been "locked up" for up to 35 years. They are creating "homes" that are truly welcoming for people who the "system" said could never be "released." It's working beautifully. We also had two wonderful days working in a botanical garden – in Chilliwack – with a school system that is making excellent efforts to welcome all children. We managed my nephew's birthday and a Mother's Day dinner (which mum cooked) before transiting through Toronto en route to England.

We changed clothes, and flew to Manchester, England – on May 14. The night we arrived, we "stayed up" to make the time adjustment, and took in the London production of GREASE. It was high energy nostalgia for the 50's – and the Manchester audience was as vibrant as the dancers. Thousands of them knew all the words and hand motions – and many spent blocks of the performance on their feet – as extensions of the stage performance. We don't know which performance we liked better, but it was a great welcome.

We worked with a Human Service agency in Oldham (greater Manchester) where Owen Cooper – a leader of the future, focused our skills in two remarkable events. One of his staff (Graham), who likely had a previous career in munitions, arranged a "BiG BanG" opening with a smoke machine and an

explosion – which (when we recovered) was exceeded by his
closing "fireworks." He had a confetti cannon – that lifted 150
people off the floor on the first shock wave, and showered
them in confetti before they could recover. All participants
survived and it was a great workshop with an amazing team.
We managed a Clannad (Irish) concert just before taking the
train to Nottingham.

In Nottingham, we now have our own private "Robin Hood
and Maid Marion" – Gerv and Sue Leyden. We stayed in their
country house – and ate, sang, walked and ran (Gerv is a runner
and I limped dutifully and painfully in his wake). Gerv organized a "singing lesson" for Marsha – and I eventually joined in.
Remarkably it was good fun – but there is definitely room for
work.

The Nottingham workshops were exhausting – and renew-
ing. The Gerv team, with Colin and Derek, crafted three events
(a day on MAPS; a day on PATH; and a huge "inclusion day"),
with 150 people in a gorgeous university conference centre
with many wonderful high tech toys. Fun was had by all. The
results are very gratifying. There really is a powerful network
of committed and skilled trainers who are making a difference
for families and children – and in a whole education system.

On our "day off" in the middle of those events, we had a
global lunch – linking our Nottingham friends with some of our
New Zealand connections who arranged lunch as part of their
UK trip. Seeing Ray Murray (from the College of Education in
Auckland) in Nottingham was serious fun – and a bit of a
mental pretzel. Ray – in Nottingham – wonderful! It is a small
world.

Marsha Forest & Jack Pearpoint

Our last night in Nottingham – after the "big event" was the Leyden traditional party. Friends, cricket on the lawn, food, great chats – and finally a musical implosion facilitated by Gerv's collection of 'hats'. Gerv and Marsha tinkled keys, Derek picked guitar, Colin slid trombone almost everywhere, and with a "rental," Jack crooned a tenor sax. No recordings will be released, but a good time was had by all.

After Nottingham, we noticed exhaustion had slipped into our lexicon – so we accepted an invitation from Mark Vaughan (CSIE in Bristol) to use their caravan on the Dorset coast (in the south of England) for three days of rest. We walked on the beaches and hills – in rain, in fog, and even in splotches of sunshine. It renewed us and reminded us of "our place" as we trudged on fields that were farmed for a millennium before the Romans came (and left); and the Normans came (and stayed); and the Spanish Armada came (and was devastated) – right in front of our caravan! And poets have written, and bombers spewed their devastation, and convoys harboured, and invasion forces gathered – all in sight of our caravan. And we walked the esplanade of Weymouth – a Victorian delight – tweaking our coaxial computer reality with simpler delights – the Punch and Judy show (next to where a new friend Andy was born) – and a man building Sand castles. Meanwhile, the 18 miles of Chisel beach roars endlessly – as it has for uncharted thousands of years – a "virtual" reminder of our insignificance. Trillions of gravel stones roll up with the onslaught of surf – and rumble back into frothing gloom – back and forth – as they did before the Romans, and through the Armada and the bomb raids, now, and for millennia yet uncharted – regardless of our plans, our PATHS, our hopes, our dreams. For us, it was soothing – being

131

one with the past, the present and the future – by just being.

Mark Vaughan, Christina Shewell and son Jack joined us for a renewal lunch – and the ceremonial "handing of the keys" to their caravan. We are counting on seeing them in Canada within the year.

Next stop – Edinburgh – with a "knockout" beginning. Heather Anderson Richie was racing to pick us up and collided with the taxi door – so we collected her at the Royal Infirmary – recovering from concussion. She survived and will be joining us in Toronto for our Summer Institute July 6-13. It was "old home" week – with the Pete Richie SHS team. Jo Kennedy persisted in staying almost through our two events – but eventually had to give in – to a greater need – the birth of her first child. Some people will use any excuse. The two workshops were successful – as were the renewals of friendships. Lizzie and Mike Hardy completed their renovations in time so we broke in their new guest room – which we commend to your attention. After the "events", the predictable gathering at Pete's covered many topics at many volumes (including a wide range of musical tastes). We were able to reconnect with Andy Muir (formerly of Swansea) and be part of the welcoming committee for our friend and colleague from Los Angeles – Laura Broderick – who will be spending the next six months with SHS in Edinburgh. Los Angeles and Edinburgh — hmmmmm... an interesting mix.

Sunday, we had brunch with George and Ethel Gray – our mentors who welcomed us to Scotland in 1979. George is as sharp as ever at 88, and Ethel grilled us gently to be sure we were still on track and making a decent living. From there, cousins and friends, Andrew & Maie Merrylees, picked us up and whisked us off to Bonkle for the last two days of our UK tour. We ate. And we spent Monday in Glasgow at the Charles Rennie Mackintosh exhibit which is stunning. He was a genius Scottish architect – decades ahead of his time – who initiated much of what we now know as art deco. The exhibit will tour New York, Chicago and LA next year. Go!

Particularly dramatic was the fact that Andrew got us a tour of **his** newest building – the Motherwell Heritage Museum. It isn't open yet – but if you are in Scotland – go – it's fabulous.

And so, as we pack up, and climb on the plane after 3 weeks in UK, we have begun the spring tour. The grass is creeping up, flowers peaking through the mulch – and we are ready for more. We will catch up briefly, then fit in workshops in Halton, Pittsburgh, Dallas, and Yellowknife before the month ends - all in time to return for our Summer Institute (at which, close to a hundred of us will have an extraordinary week of learning together – July 6-13).

And so, as we feel the warmth of the sun in Toronto and see the garden and the office, we are glad to be back – even briefly – and glad to be working hard – making a contribution. We are balancing the work with the rest days. We are enjoying our life. Our work is getting stronger and deeper. We were always thankful for each day – and now we appreciate each as unique even more. We hope you are doing the same.

So, write, call, drop in – stay connected.. If you don't have a copy of our new *Inclusion News*, we printed 70,000 and over half are out. Don't wait, ask now. And if you can surf the net, be sure to check our Web Page: **http://inclusion.com**

Dream Catchers and Dolphins

Have a great Summer!

Jack & Marsha
June 6, 1996

January 27, **1997**

Life Support Required... Again

Dearest Friends,

I have been deliberating for days about whether to send this letter. It hasn't been an easy decision. It feels like years ago, but on Jan.9 during my routine three month medical check, my wonderful and careful medical oncologist, Michael Crump, found a tiny lump in my left breast. Moving quickly we went across the road to Mt. Sinai Hospital where my breast disease doctor, Irv Koven, did a needle biopsy. The results were inconclusive so, Irv scheduled an ultrasound needle biopsy (Jan. 14) which confirmed cancer cells (Jan. 16th)! Shock!

From there, I was scheduled to meet a new surgeon, Irv's associate, Dr. Saul Sidlofsky. The first available appointment was Tues. Jan. 21. I saw him, and was scheduled for surgery on Feb. 3. During the pre-op workup, on Jan. 27, they also found a suspicious lymph node in my abdominal area. More shock!

We have another day of tests on Monday Jan. 27 (bone scan and CAT scan) and then we will hopefully fly to Winnipeg to work Tuesday through Sunday. Home Sunday. Surgery Monday. Winnipeg will be a blessed distraction, as well as great work and our friends there will take good and loving care of us.

Here are the possible scenarios:

1. Intraductal breast cancer like I had 8 years ago. The surgery is relatively simple and, as a protocol, is followed by radiation. This is what we hope for. They can only determine this from

a biopsy done during the surgery on Feb.3.

2. Invasive breast cancer. If this is the case, they remove more tissue and some of the underarm lymph nodes. They install drainage tubes. Then we wait. The tests on the lymph nodes could take two weeks to determine what is what. This is not our favourite option, as then chemo or other treatment will be discussed.

3. The abdominal lymph node issue also will be investigated. We will see what happens on that front.

All in all, we are shocked and upset. We are up and down. We are sad and mad and scared. Our mentor and guide in New Zealand, Uncle Whitu, as well as Te Ripowai, urges us to keep working and keep living our lives. Shafik in Philadelphia has been amazing in his wisdom and insights. He is the one who truly encouraged me to send this letter (along with John O'Brien, who is here for the week-end working with us on new plans for *Inclusion Press)*.

I have been afraid to tell people. Afraid they would stop asking us to work. Afraid they would treat me as sick. Afraid I would be bothering people. Sure I should do it alone, etc., etc. Shafik keeps telling me how much people care about me and Jack and that I need everyone's prayers, chants, songs, warrior energy, blood sacrifices (that's O'Brien's humour kicking in). In other words, do what it takes to send me and us all your good and heartfelt energy to lick this disease and get it out of my system so that we can carry on our lives.

Shafik writes, "Marsha, share your reality and say what you

need and what you don't need. Let us be with you. Remind people (so you can carry on your work) that you are not sick, just medically challenged (smile). You are not sick, my Thunder (Shafik calls me *Thunder* and Jack *Lightening*), you are simply being delayed."

Shafik also wisely advises that "the doctors will assist in this greatly, but the main victory lies within your village and ultimately within yourself (your most spiritual connection.) Look in the mirror Thunder and see that warrior that is you. Now go and have some fun!!!!"

I must admit the fun part is hard to do but we went out to Shopsy's for great corned beef sandwiches and then had a buying spree at a great bookstore. It was fun!

We are definitely planning to continue our schedule; to make our video in Yellowknife; to do our courses; and to scuba dive a lot more.

OK – I need you all. I need every ounce of good and healthy energy to get me and Jack through all this. Jack will have Gary Bunch with him at the hospital along with Rose.

That's all. We will advise you of what is happening.

Please respect our boundaries.

1. We just don't have the energy to talk to everyone so we would rather you e-mailed or faxed. If you feel you must call, make it short.

Dreamcatchers and Dolphins

2. Please do not send flowers. Books and other stuff are fine, but please no books about cancer or sickness. Stuff about health and healing and laughter and adventure and life!!

3. Don't treat me as sick. Treat me as healthy. The definition of health is the ability to deal with this kind of shit. I am fortunately healthy enough to fight this. However, it is not easy, believe me!!

4. This is a family affair. Illness like this hits the family, in this case me and Jack – so include him in your thoughts and prayers.

5. I don't want to hear that this 'illness is a choice' and 'you can control your life if you want to.' Trust me, I didn't **choose** this! However, I am choosing how to **deal with** it. I alternatively want to hide in a cave and to fight like hell. I will, with your help, fight like hell – for again as Shafik writes, "I know one of the hardest things during times like this is to wait. Do the things you really like to do as you wait. Get on people's nerves if you must, but don't dare to go it alone...never go it alone."

This sounds like the stuff we say: "Together We're Better" and all that... and yet I hesitated to write because to write means it is real.

I believe in the power of all of you out there to send in your own unique ways your healing energy and spirit. I need you. There I said it. I did it. Now John and Jack will press the magic buttons and send it.

138

There is a song dear Gerv taped for me in England. It is a song that I heard in my head as I walked along the road in Nottingham, as I will again this May. It is "I WILL SURVIVE!!" and I'll add the song that now spins in my head. It is called "I get by with a little help with my friends........"

Thank you in advance for respecting my boundaries and sending your hearts and healing energy our way.

Much love.

Marsha   - and of course also Jack.

Dreamcatchers and Dolphins

Dear Thunder (the louder one)

I am writing to share with you some thoughts that *remained* with me after we talked last week. I write (as did the wise woman of the village) saying to you from the very beginning, "I will only teach you what you already know." I am responding to your sadness and your discouragement about the fact that some days you feel so fine, as if you have finally turned the corner ... and then comes that next day ... and you're somewhat at the beginning again, not feeling very "up."

Thunder, my world is very much like this too. In fact, though I started this letter (and wrote most of it) to you last evening (Sunday), I am adding to it at 4:43 am Monday morning. I turned on my computer at 3:57 am this morning on my way back from the bathroom. Because I was once again experiencing the **D-Zone** (feeling dizziness, disorientation and *dis-ease*), I couldn't get to my computer which is less than 4 feet from my bed until the 4:43 am time (46 minutes later). I laid there in my bed, once again afraid to get up because getting up meant having to deal with the fact that I'd probably be off balance and could therefore fall. So I laid there waiting and waiting until I felt safe enough to try getting up again and leaving the D-Zone. Yes, I could have gotten someone to help me get back up. I simply decided to wait the D-Zone out this time. Why am I mentioning this? Because when I went to bed last night, the D-Zone was nowhere to be found. I went to bed feeling real good having just returned from Michigan. I went to bed feeling great. I woke up in the D-Zone. I too ask myself, "when will I turn the corner?" I raise these things Thunder to "raise" you a little. Thunder, what you feel is real. Allow yourself to accept the reality of your feelings. Be angry if you must. Shut down if you must. These are legitimate responses to not feeling good consistently. Almost every night I lay in my bed feeling pretty satisfied about what I *did* that day; and almost every night I lay in my bed feeling pretty upset about how I *felt* that day. Interesting isn't it?

First Divide: Then Unite

Thunder, our cancer is *not* a friend to us. It does not embrace us lovingly, nor does it exist so as to make us comfortable, or cheerful, or to make us smile, or **regularly** feel good. It will not sing harmonious rhythms to us, nor will it allow us to often feel powerful. But we will smile anyway, and be powerful anyway, and we will sing and dance sometimes despite our cancer and its dangerous treatments (chemo-therapy, radiation, etc.). We will do these things despite the cancer because we have companions and friends who will give us every single thing we need to feel "up" at the necessary times.

Thunder, on a hospital heart monitor, is not the line of life both up *and* down? Is not death one straight boring line? Loved one, you can not be "up" at all times. Life involves the unity of opposites!!! It is somewhat like birth. With every new joyous birth, is there not some degree of pain? Even with the greatness of the sun, can it prevent the rain? We just are not going to be "up" all the time. Life isn't like that, and can't be like that. Thunder, I feel very "okay" at times and I'd like it to stay that way. However, I now accept the reality that I can't be that way **always;** I can't even be that way a lot anymore.

Dreamcatchers and Dolphins

Thunder, I hope you come to accept that "**Not Feeling Good**" consistently is going to be your reality, probably up to the point of your death. As for me, when my death comes, and if given the opportunity, I intend to embrace it with open arms and a welcoming smile. I accept my death as one of the most certain things about my life, maybe the *most* sure thing we know about life. In that you are concerned about your death, allow me to say, Thunder, that your death will be yet another stage of your development. It will be sort of like Martin's death, and Malcolm's death. The more we try to bury them, the more we give them life. Have you noticed that?

A young man in my youth group told me he would never forget me (for the impact I've had on his life). If this pledge remains true for him, did he not just guarantee me everlasting life – that I will always be? You Marsha Forest will forever be!!! Yes, my sister, you do have much more to do; and you are really enjoying your life right now and you don't want this enjoyment to end. Well, guess what?

Somebody told me that "people prepared to die don't easily die." Chill out Thunder!!! Enjoy what you presently have and leave tomorrow to tomorrow.

Now why am I writing to you like this? Please know Thunder that I am only willing to speak to you about death because you spoke to me about it. Since you raise it with me occasionally, I raise it back with you. I am not willing to pretend these concerns are not front and foremost on your mind. You make it clear to me that they are. I sincerely apologize if I have in any way scared you or upset you, but I take the position that you are holding too much of this stuff inside. This, to me, only creates more **dis**-*ease* (out of ease-ness). I hope I have not overstepped my bounds, but in the village in which I live and represent, I am taught that if I can not tell the *whole* truth, I am to tell nothing. As an African warrior, **I Do Not Have The Right To Remain Silent!!!**

Remember Thunder, our greatest and most effective cancer treatment is our human support systems, our village mates, our community!!! It takes a whole village to defeat one tumor. Continue to develop your systems of support. Also, remember that it is your right, in fact, it is much more that your right, it is your *responsibility* to decide who and when you will allow others to enter your "cancer" space. Share what you will, when you so choose. But when you share, dear Thunder, share the *whole* truth, or share nothing. Don't fear sharing your whole story (your fears, doubts, let-downs, etc.). We all have them and they need not be hidden. If you only release a partial picture, you'll only get partial support. Relax upon us Thunder, relax upon me. We are your most effective cure!!! If you build it (Trust) .. we will come!!

From your brother and co-thinker,

Shafik

Dreamcatchers and Dolphins

 Peace be with you Thunder ...

Thank you for sharing your concerns with me. I really understand your fear Thunder, I really do. I hope that you know this. Feel your fear Thunder ... but don't stay there. You know that I believe that people should embrace their cancer "visits". I've told you this before. I have a different challenge for you this time. Don't embrace it ... confront it. I know you are tired of this, Thunder, but remember that life is "up" and "down" (see any heart monitor). You need to look in the mirror and remember that you are a warrior. Warriors run to the war, not from it. Look in the mirror and remember that you/we can defeat this.

I know that one of the hardest things during times like this is the waiting, isn't it!! Nevertheless, you'll have to. Do the things you really like to do as you wait, okay? Get on people's nerves if you must, but don't dare try to go it alone... never go it alone.

Thunder, identify your fears/concerns. Say to yourself (or write them down) what they are. We can defeat those things that we are clear about. It is confusion that feeds dis-ease. Figure out your fears, Thunder; identify them and then eliminate them. The doctors will assist in this, but the main victory lies within your village and ultimately within yourself (your most spiritual connection). Look in the mirror Thunder, and see that warrior that is you. Now go have some fun !!!!!!

Shafik

 Thunder (the louder one),

It is 4:22am (Friday morning) and since I couldn't sleep, I decided to answer some "mail". Marsha, it was so good to hear your THUNDER!! Keep it loud.

Yes, yes, yes !!! Let us be with you. Share your reality and continue to say what you need; and more importantly, what you don't need. Remind people (so you can still get hired) that YOU ARE NOT SICK ... just medically challenged (smile). You are not sick, my Thunder, you are simply being delayed.

Marsha, you asked about "The Village". This is how I remember the story :

> "Come to the edge" he said.
> They said, "We are afraid !!!"
> "Come to the edge" he said.
> They came ... he pushed them,
> They flew !!!!

We are ready to gently guide you to the edge, but your flying is up to you. You and Lightning have taken many to the edge (after having "trained" them to fly). You were able to teach them how to fly because you are good at flying. Now go flap your wings. Lightning will flap his and together you will soar as high as you so need ... or as high as you think you can (it's up to you !!!). If however you get tired, or find yourself going down, your village will be there to catch you both ... trust us !!!!

Peace be with you both,
Shafik   (one who has been caught)

145

On The Edge

January 26, 1997

Shafik, dearest dearest friend,

I am on the edge. You are brilliant and sending all the right stuff. Today was really hard but the e-mail and faxes are coming in. Richard Rosenberg was first and he said we were booked for CalTASH, Spring 1998. He was terrific. Everyone is truly out there and I am awed. This morning I was floored and the telephone not working just sent me right over the cliff.

Tomorrow is hospital day, again (bone scans and CAT scans), and hopefully we will fly away for sanity work in Winnipeg on Tues.

This is not easy. I do trust you (saying) that the village is there to catch us both. And I know that you speak from far too much experience.

I hope you and Shina are OK. Please let us know so we can send our Thunder and Lightening energy to you too.

Shafik, you got me through a very rough week-end. I never take friendship and love for granted. I deeply appreciate your love. And we will be at your wedding with buttons and bows and bells. We will have a blow out in Philly at the end of May. Send me the date again so I can be sure to book our England tickets around your wedding.

Much much much love and hugs and vulnerability (since you think it is so adorable)

Marsha and Jack

Dear Marsha and Jack:

As hard as it was for you to write your note, please know that I am very grateful for the opportunity to join in the chorus of prayers. I am an absolute believer in the power of collective thought and collective prayer. My voice has joined the choir. In an odd way you, by your e-mail, showed the importance of inclusion and demonstrated that inclusion means acceptance and being surrounded by people, but at the same time the establishment of sacred space. I have always seen boundaries as being a way of creating a sacred place that allowed me to plant my deepest thoughts into untrampled soil. Boundaries are my fences ... there is a sign on them that says, "I love you, but keep your fucking feet off my garden."

So, do you like books on tape? I travel so much that I buy "books" and pop them into the cassette recorder, in the car, and let someone read to me. – so if you could use them, let me know. I hesitate to admit this but they are mostly murder mysteries and the like ... who needs Shakespeare when driving the 401? I also admit to watching the *Young and the Restless* ... ok ok enough with the disclosure.

Dave Hingsburger

Dreamcatchers and Dolphins

January 26, 1997

Chorus

Dear Dave,

Thanks for your speedy response. Today was a tough day. Should I have sent that letter? What will they think? I exposed myself. Oi oi oi. But it was a good choice and already the energy is flowing in and I need it, and Jack needs it, and in fact we all need it. Welcome to the chorus. I am pleased and honoured you are on board my circle of life.

I loved you boundary thing especially the part about "keep your fucking feet off my garden." Got a good laugh out of that. Thanks.

No thanks by the way re the books on tape. I have armed myself with reading as I can really lose myself in books. I too love a great greasy mystery and although I don't like soaps, I do love ER, Chicago Hope, Murder One, etc.

We will get through this with a little help from our friends.

Much love.
Marsha and Jack

Marsha Forest & Jack Pearpoint

Marsha,

It's January 31, 5:15 pm as I read your e-mail. Girl, I will have you in my thoughts and prayers. Being raised Catholic, it's hard to get away from thinking of lighting candles and saying the rosary. Although I may end up doing both of those, I offer my Nia in celebration of your health (a form of mind/body/spirit expression – through movement and dance). In performing Nia, I am most powerfully awake and most fully who I am. I will participate in 3 classes before we go with you into surgery on Monday: 2 Saturday morning and one Sunday morning. I will dance in your name, in celebration of your health and your intention to keep it, and in the name of Jack, whose life is so closely entwined in your own. I will dance strength, joy, energy, love and healing to you, and to Jack and Dr. Paul, as they will need the same, in different ways.

I respect your boundaries. When I think of you, I think of you as robust and healthy. I will look around for some good tunes this weekend to send your way.

Jack, you can e-mail here or call me if there is something I can do or say or listen to you say, that will help. You are both in my focus. Inform us when you can, and put every ounce of your intention into living this moment and many years into the foreseeable future.

To the universe I say: "I am Charlene Comstock-Galagan. I stand in recognition of Marsha Forest. Her intention is to live. I witness her life and I take her intention as my own, adding my power to her own. We gather and focus the intention of each one in her village, adding their power to our own. We will be heard and not misunderstood. We send our intention on the winds, in the four directions, above us and below us.

149

Dream Catchers and Dolphins

We invoke the fire power of the sun, the magnetic force of the moon, and every force of earth and sky to strengthen the power of our intention, which we speak aloud, clearly, and in love. We choose life. Amen."

Charlene

Marsha Forest & Jack Pearpoint

Marsha and Jack,

Hang on, hold on, hang in –

We are praying and hoping for you. I understand the "oh shit" reaction. People will tell you
how brave you are, but we know that there are really few
choices, right? Brave or what?

I do advise something crazy and distracting — perhaps a
bungie jump off the CN tower? - or -"Cancer sucks" graffiti
scrawled on buildings in spray paint? More soon. WE love you.

I will send healing light this morning to overpower the CAT
scan and bone scan and erase negative images from the body
and the film.

Lots of love, Mara S.

Dreamcatchers and Dolphins

Marsha

What to say? There are no words.
What to do? I feel so helpless.
How to react?

To tell you that you are brave and strong and wonderful and that you can overcome this. And above all to tell you that you are not alone. Marsha and Jack, there will be people all over the world pulling for you. And you, of all people, should know what a difference that makes.

As you can see I'm back at work after my own ordeal. I can truly say however, that so many wonderful things happened, and so many gifts were offered — that I would never have known if I hadn't had a brain tumour — that it was NOT a negative experience, and I ALMOST don't even wish that it hadn't happened. Almost, mind you — my face is paralyzed on one side but with faith and time I am confident that "this too shall pass."

Jack, as you support Marsha, may others also support you. We'll be praying and waiting for the news of your triumph.

Barb H.

Marsha Forest & Jack Pearpoint

Good day, Marsha —

A couple of weeks ago I was driving around doing errands in the middle of the day, half listening to the local jazz station on the car radio. As a change of pace, I sometimes tune in to Dr. Laura Schlesinger, because even old self-centered hedonists find moral certainty appealing, if not persuasive. She is intolerant of rationalization, even the well-honed, advanced form I practice. I figure she and I could never be friends. Do you get nationally-syndicated Dr. L. up north? But I digress. I was listening to the music, and thinking about other stuff, when a song came on whose lyrics penetrated the distractions. The tune was Latinesque, kinda Brazilian-bouncy. It would remind you of the soundtrack behind a B-movie from South America or maybe Italy. But the chorus went like this:

> In a circle of friends
> In a circle of sound
> All our voices will blend
> When we touch common ground.

Listening I thought to myself, with everything else Marsha has to deal with, when did she find time to write the lyrics to a jazz tune? It's funny how often I think of you and the lessons I have learned from you (going back what, fifteen, eighteen years?) Take yesterday. I was with a group of a half dozen people who represent four organizations that have created a little coalition we call "Californians for Inclusive Education." The purpose is to establish a lobbying presence in the state legislature and regulatory bodies on behalf of inclusive schooling. Ann Halvorsen from Cal-TASH was there, as was

153

Dream Catchers and Dolphins

Diane Lipton from DREDF (you'll remember she was the attorney who fought the Rachel Holland case), someone from the state protection and advocacy agency, and a fellow named Tom Neary and I from the Supported Life Institute, here in Sacramento. We were talking about the individuals we had just interviewed for the part-time lobbyist position we created with monies and in-kind raked from the meager coffers of our various groups. We were discussing what positions we'd want the person to represent. As we talked, it dawned on me that our thinking had somehow drifted back to the point where "inclusive schooling" was being defined a **classroom** experience – a placement option. At a certain point, the Voice of Marsha rang in my ears and I went off on a rant about inclusion and the school **community** experience. "Let's get back to what Marsha taught us a long time ago," I sputtered. The discussion, which had jumped the track, righted itself and we gained better clarity about our message. That sort of thing – hearing the Voice of Marsha – happens a lot to me. I guess that's the mark of a great teacher: the lessons, the way of thinking about things, become our touchstones and last a lifetime. The great Teachers in my life I can count on the fingers of one hand and one finger of the other hand. By order of appearance, they are: Aaron Brownstein, Og Lindsley, Marc Gold, Wolf Wolfensberger, John O'Brien, and Marsha Forest. How fortunate I have been for having such marvellous teachers. Your lessons, though, have a unique quality.

Unless a piano drops from the sky and squishes the both of us, the odds are good that Kay or I – and then together – will at some point have to enter the struggle against a life-threatening cancer. How we face it may be different, but you and Jack have prepared us (and many, many others) with lessons of courage

154

and honesty that we will come back to in moments of despair and gain strength to go on. The chronicles you and Jack have shared with those of us on your list have been moving, but more important, helpful. I wonder if you had that purpose in mind. Maybe teaching is a habit. In any case, your sharing will help us when it comes our turn. I haven't known what to say to you before.

I am not good at words that comfort or bolster spirits. And not knowing what to say, I have said little. But I have read, and I have listened. And finally it dawned on me what to say. Simply – thanks for the lessons. You will always be one of the fingers that have taught me how to think about things. Here's hoping you'll keep the lessons flowing for a long time to come.

You'll be in my thoughts next Monday.

Love, Charlie G.

Dreamcatchers and Dolphins

Hi Guys!!!
It seems like yesterday
that we were chatting
out in the sunshine
on the streets of New Orleans.
A breath of Spring
in what should have been Winter
enjoying the Company
of those Others that Love as we do.
energized by our Village
that has grown and grown
United in our passions and hopes
pursuing our dreams of a World
where the Individual is Valued
as part of the Whole
that Love is yours
so, it is good that you reach out
and surround yourself
with what we have freely given
a lit candle glows
with light and warmth
but, it casts shadows as well
that is the nature of all things
your candle is lit
it glows and is warm
we send our Light to you
to send the shadows
into the far corners
we send our Love
to support your Glow

Hugs and Kisses, Mark P.

Marsha Forest & Jack Pearpoint

Dear Marsha and Jack

Many prayers, filled with spirit and light and dancing and joy. May your heart be full, not afraid. I want to share this poem with you that I wrote in 1970.

The Fall and the Rescue

It is this that is the beginning
that reaching out and hoping
to touch another,
the brief tremor of the inner smile
that burns a realness deep within.
When in terror and desperation
horror sinking and screaming
and empty and oh so lost from home
I jump to far below
the deathly, agonizing coldness
cushioning air
falling
Oh God !! I'm hurting!

And then there are arms
reaching out and picking me up
soft but strong
loving
falling dizziness and tension
taken by security
the enfolding, encircling
protecting cushion of those
who love and care.

Dream Catchers and Dolphins

Thinking of you and your circle and what you are dealing with right now these words came to mind.

May the God of Victory, Love be with you.

Michael P.

Dearest Marsha and Jack,

– Surgery Tomorrow –

I send prayers and healing light and hope and power. And I send love. Lots of love. I agree that cancer is no gift. But the love is the gift.

And I love watching you take it into your heart. It is yours to keep.

Mara S.

Dreamcatchers and Dolphins

Dear Marsha and Jack,

I added my prayers to the thousands of others who held you in their hearts yesterday and who will continue to do so.

You are writing and telling about one of life's most important moments. Your list of do's and don'ts was most helpful – it could be given to pastoral ministers and hospital chaplains for reprint!　　A favourite phrase of mine (in those times when I couldn't control my life the way that I wanted to do) is from Dag Hammerjold (sp): "We are not permitted to choose the framework of our destiny." It comes back to me now. You teach me and so many about inclusion. But, now you are teaching in a different arena – one that you did not choose. You are effective, even here.　I will continue to pray for you.

For now, remember that you are both loved and that prayers are storming our God who must be saying, "Who is this person, anyway?" – because of all the e-mails to heaven! Well, we know who this person is – the bringer of hope and the changer of systems. We need you – so follow all of the good advice that you are getting and Get Well!

Love,
Marilyn　B.

February 2, 1997

Surgery Tomorrow...

Dearest *Whanau* (this word in Maori means
extended family and you out there are indeed our
extended family),

We are overwhelmed by the beauty and power of the
messages of support we are getting daily. They are more than
we ever could have wanted or expected. Keep them coming.
They are healing. They are helpful. They are treasures.

We are in Winnipeg. It is Sunday morning after an incredible
three day event with 45 mostly aboriginal people and their
friends in the health care and community education stuff. What
an amazing group to be with. You can tell that they were not
feeling "sorry" for us as they stayed till the very last drop
yesterday. They are loving the tools – MAPS, PATH, CIRCLES*.
They understand them from a deep deep place of hurt and pain
and grief. They are also committed to "doing – not whining"
for this generation and the next seven to follow. This has been
the right place to be this week.

It seems I am surrounded by wise and loving mentors and
friends. I asked my friend Josie Hill before the workshop,
"What should I do? Should I tell people what is going on with
my cancer?" Josie, a warrior woman, a metis, a woman who
has, as she describes it, been through it all and then some, said
the same words as Shafik, as John O'Brien, and as loving Jack
said: "YES!"

* MAPS, PATH & CIRCLES are planning tools developed by Jack, Marsha,
John O'Brien & others - to support individuals & families. See the order
form at the back of the book for brief descriptions of books and videos.

Dream Catchers and Dolphins

Josie put it this way: "If you don't tell people, you will hurt them. They will pick up that something is wrong, and they will think it is their fault, or that you are angry with them. Just tell them – and carry on."

So I did. With the flute of Carlos Nakai in the background, I told my truth. I also said that I had a circle, that I didn't want advice, that I, and we, wanted their support and love...

Did we get it? You bet we did!

And the workshop was astounding in its energy and power. Their PATHS were fantastic. Colour and music and energy filled the room.

When Jack and I did the *Circle of Friends* piece, we spoke of all of you and the messages we are receiving. Yes, there are lessons to be learned here and we are learning them. I do not, and will not, see the cancer as a gift. I do however see the experience as one that has many lessons to teach and I am listening to the lessons.

I have deep moments of terror and despair. I am in terrible anguish when I think of the pain I am causing Jack and those who love me, but I did not choose this cancer. I can only choose how to act now and to maximize my and Jack's possibility to survive this with dignity, with moments of joy, with hours of fear and with the knowledge that we are truly loved. That is the gift. I really don't need any more reminders of this, but life is as it is. So that is that and we deal with it.

Yesterday, I almost fell apart at lunch waiting for Jack to call the hospital to confirm the surgery and to find out if any tests came back re the mystery lymph node. After another long wait, the surgery was confirmed (AMEN) but the doctor was away (who has or doesn't have the lymph node results). So I came up with a way to survive my quandary of what to worry about first. You are all allowed to laugh at this slogan I coined. "First the breast, then worry about the rest." Josie, Jack and I cracked up. I took a half a Xanax (my little pill when I get over stressed) and we continued the workshop with flair.

There is no other choice. I can't worry any more. I am worried out. So last night, Jack and Nerina and John and I had wine and ribs and trimmings.

We had a fire. I finished a trashy novel and tomorrow we fly back to Toronto for surgery.

Josie has also advised me that one of her elders told her to tell me to talk to my body and not **ask** it, but **tell** it to be well. I said, "Please?" – and Josie said "**NO** please! Just tell your body out loud. This cancer thing is aggressive – so talk to it FIRMLY.   **NO** please."

So I do. Why not? This is **warrior** time, Josie reminded me. This is time for the sharks not the dolphins. Better yet, this is time for the dolphins, turtles and sharks to gather these offending cancers and take them way way far away. You all can sweep or chant or sing or pray. Anything in any way is welcome. And for me, the lesson is not to pray for me to get well and to run off selfishly, and become a scuba diver (tempting I must admit). The lesson is to get well, so Jack and I can continue to speak and write and share these amazing lessons we are learning. It seems to really be making an impact.

In this world of self reliance, independence and "me", I am

really learning to believe in the "WE".

One e-mail from our dear friend in Yellowknife, Hugh Lloyd, really hit me in the eyes. Hugh is married to Elisip, an amazing Inuit woman from Igloolik. Previously, she had gently told us the stories of her youth including tales that you don't want to hear. Tales of pain and sickness. Also tales of community and connectedness. Tales of friendship and tales of denial. The whole thing.

Hugh was recently travelling with Elisip's brother George, and they were chatting about Jack and my situation (Isn't that beautiful said Josie Hill that they were talking about you and sharing that talk with you). YES...

Anyway, George was patiently explaining to Hugh that the word INUK has far more meaning than the way white folks interpret it as meaning "a person".

It is used to describe the occupier or possessor of space. All things are possessed with spirit...people, rocks, plants, everything has a spirit.

They raised my e-mail letter. George told Hugh that "Inuk share information of all sorts with each other in a BOLD and public way." George told Hugh: "It is selfish to hold things within oneself and not to share them with others. Keeping things hidden causes oneself to suffer and makes it harder for all the connected ones to know and share and help. Just as the Inuit were usually very generous with food, and shelter and the small number of material things they had, so too they were generous with what we split off as the spiritual side of life."

I love this. I needed validation that sending the e-mail, speaking my pain and my fear was really OK to do. I am not recommending it to anyone else. I am simply stating that, for me, all your messages of support, your humour, your tears, your honestly – are getting me into surgery in at least one piece. I feel surrounded by a chorus of love. It counteracts the fear and terror of dying – for basically this is what it's all about. Shout it loud and clear. I am terrified of dying. I love my life, my work, my friends, my wonderful JACK. But I, like everyone of you, don't know what tomorrow will bring. Sheila Jupp taught me that. And Sheila would say, in her beautiful and gentle and strong way, "Do what it takes to live." And I am!

Thank you all. Thank you deeply and magnificently for who each of you is. Your voices are coming through loud and clear and each is unique and each is the same.

Time for the lovely dinner upstairs. We will write again after the surgery. This is an incredible ordeal. I would prefer that it was not happening. But it is. You are all making it bearable. You are being friends in the truest sense of the word and I end with another Maori word that Te Ripowai taught me.

Arohanui (big love)

I will write more after the surgery....That's a promise to me and to all of you.

Marsha

and now a word from *Jack*

Dream Catchers and Dolphins

Yesterday, at the workshop ended – we passed Marsha's greenstone around the room as a "talking stone" – so each person had a moment to say whatever they chose. One after another, people teased the pain and anguish of families they know – and said they now had tools to help build a future for the children. We were definitely in the right place this week. And then we received gifts – eagle feather goblets, and hand crafted pins – and a Star Blanket one of the women had just made. The blanket will be there, with the warmth of well-wishing from Winnipeg, to wrap Marsha right after the surgery.

And a special thanks to Nerina and John – who encompassed us and took care of us all week here in Winnipeg. We were tired – and tense and they "mothered" us wonderfully. We are ready to return – and face tomorrow...

Tomorrow (Monday) at 11:30...

Jack

Marsha Forest & Jack Pearpoint

Marsha

A prayer is a wish the heart makes. This morning I rose a little early, I have to travel today but I wanted to sit a bit in the quiet. The country can be quiet. With snow blanketing the ground and morning cold and dark keeping those of feather and fur nested, there is silence. It is only in true quiet that I can catch my breath and allow myself to reflect. In the hush this morning I think of Marsha and her ordeal of endurance and Jack's ordeal of helpless waiting. In the quiet, one realizes that words are often just noise that fills silence borne of not knowing what to say. Noise that masks our inability to really do something. Noise that makes us feel better about inadequacy. Years ago I was afraid of silence. I filled it with all sorts of noise, something about the quiet scared me. Now I realize that I was afraid of the absolute power of silence. I was afraid of the journey that silence would bid me take. I was afraid of who I was in silence. But, I've grown and am growing, comfortable with silence. And it was in that comfort, this morning, that I sought the quiet and traveled in to where I could utter a name to the cosmos. The name I uttered was "Marsha." In silence I joined with others. In silence, we join with you. In silence our hearts make a wish . . . and we pray.

God Speed, Holy Strength, Powerful Silence.

Dave Hingsburger

Dreamcatchers and Dolphins

Dear Marsha and Jack,

So many thoughts and emotions, but just want to continue offering tons of support. The way I do that best, when I am scared (and, yes, I am), is thinking of things that calm me. And so today I continue to send you visualizations of the place in my heart and mind that serves to calm me more than any others...my beautiful island. The symbols for me are the warmth, colors, and sounds... but since the two of you have met my island, I've added some new symbols that equate to belonging: bubbles, the beach hut, hot tubs, and cozy, comfy cuddly wearables. For me and the rest of the world, each life that you two touch expands the meaning of life for that person. Candles will be lit tonight and I will blow bubbles. Small, but it's what I can do...and I need to do something.

I love you both.

Anne

Marsha and Jack,

My silence is my support. Gifts (material gifts), flowers and poetry I could never do. I am here and I think of you often and all that you are imparting to people even at this time, which I am sure is stressful to you.

Courage is what I learn from this experience of yours. I pray for both of you and am a great believer in positive thinking. It has the power to make things happen. So let us all think positive, each one of us, and create an energy around us. Prayer and laughter.

Take care both of you. And I thank you for considering me your extended family, it is an honor.

Reena W.

Dreamcatchers and Dolphins

Dear Marsha and Jack,

This note is a little overdue, but Danny and I wanted to send you our good vibes to be an added source of healing for Marsha! I found in a magazine I was skimming through about 2 months ago a profound message written by a woman who had battled with cancer..it read:

"I am no longer afraid of mirrors where I see the sign of the amazon, the one who shoots arrows. There was a fine line across my chest where a knife entered, but now a branch winds about the scar and travels from arm to heart. Green leaves cover the branch, grapes hang there and a bird appears. What grows in me now is vital and does not cause me harm. I think the bird is singing. I have designed my chest with the care given to an illuminated manuscript. I am no longer ashamed to make love. Love is a battle I can win. I have the body of a warrior who does not kill or wound. On the book of my body, I have permanently inscribed a tree."

Marsha you are the warrior who has gone into battle as a woman, who believes in life and all that is precious (our children). It is time for us to lend you our strength for your battle for inclusion. To win the right for your body to be part of life (yours, Jack's and everyone you have touched). Danny and I will be thinking of both of you and not to worry (even through -35 degree Alberta weather) our strong vibes will find you no matter where you are.

Love Bev, Danny Ray and our kids!!!!

170

Warrior Woman,

Your spirit flows out to us all and weaves us together with the most powerful forces of love, truth and all that is real to human life.

In your honesty and realness of fear, terror and strength, you have created the opening for the power of "we" to be present with you... and with each other.

My love, prayer and demand for your body to heal is with you and Jack, and with the community of all our souls and spirits that have joined... because of your great strength and your absolute terror in being real and reaching out.

Healing and love to you and Jack,

Darleen S.

Dreamcatchers and Dolphins

 Warrior woman.

Brave woman.

Lovely woman.

I love you. And as I read your note I almost felt the earth shake. I feel your power, and that of all your friends, reverberating in my body as I sit and type. Powerful vibes are out there tonight – for you, our friend.

Love
Sharon   G.

Jack and Marsha,

Jack, I will be thinking of you today. Marsha too, for sure, but you are the spouse who is waiting by...wishing you could take it away. Peace. I hope that it goes as well as it possibly can go. For thinking of the future, and the connectedness of us all, from a whole new direction, have you seen the writings of Margaret Wheatley, one book called *"Leadership and the New Science, Learning About Organization from an Orderly Universe"*. A very interesting book, with profound implications for the ways most services are run...and fascinating since it comes from a whole new direction...There is a follow-up which I have not read called *"A Simpler Way."*

But your stacks of 'things to read for a rainy day, or a slower time,' are probably huge.

Take good care of yourselves, and thank you both for being willing to share the journey. It is and was the right thing to do.

Shalom,

Bill G.

Dreamcatchers and Dolphins

Marsha

William and I are doing our prayer-equivalents for you, Marsha. We don't ever seem to get together over the computer so I'm writing this.

When my mom was very sick in Oct, we had such a variety of messages: "I'm praying for you", "I'm thinking good thoughts for you", "I'm lighting a candle for you"... I liked the last option.

When I was in Bulgaria last year, I went to a cathedral in Varna and, despite my agnosticism, I lit candles for William, my mom, and Oksana's mom. Interesting that all three had bad times after that but all have made remarkable comebacks.

I have a big white candle in my office that will burn for days and days in your honour. Oksana says all I have to do is wish for your recovery and let the candle burn down until the wish is granted. I don't know if I'd put that above your medical help, but there's something lovely about it.

Love and strength
Ron & William

174

Marsha,

You are on my mind and in my heart every moment. Yesterday at 11:00 I stopped and meditated.

As everyone, I have experienced much loss, grief, fear and pain in my life. I have always spent much energy and effort meditating and praying for guidance, love, money, purpose, health, death, etc. After I lost my family, my prayers seemed so empty, and I realized that what I needed, more than all the laundry list of things in my prayers, was peace around all those issues. I realize that my life will bring many trials, tribulations and unrequested journeys; and each day, I pray that in the center of them all, I have peace. And in the realization that with a lot of work, support, prayer and meditation I am capable of replacing each fear with peace, I have found much strength and a tremendous freedom. As life is a never ending journey, peace has become my never ending prayer.

You have much work left to do, and so many of us need you. We need to share your knowledge and experiences. I've asked my angels to rally around you, and grab others along the way to do the same. In my Monday meditation, I pictured you both surrounded by angels.

I send you loving, healing positive energy. But most of all, I send you peace.

My love to you both.
Melissa M.

Dreamcatchers and Dolphins

February 3, 1997

Redouble Your Efforts:
It Ain't Over Till Its Over

Evening - after the surgery.

Marsha's Message as she wheels out of surgery:
"Redouble your efforts with prayers, chants, songs, etc."
" We ain't done yet! It ain't over till its over!!! " "There is
work to do..."

We don't have a lot of information yet – and it will be
another week before we get the lab results from today's surgery.
The "surgery" went well technically – and a malignant "invasive"
tumour was removed (cleanly). With invasive cancer, to
determine if it has spread, the procedure is to remove some of
the under-arm lymph nodes and send them for testing (which
takes a week).

We don't have extensive post-operative information; it isn't
our first choice. And, we still don't have the CT scan results,
but in keeping with our motto going in, "first the breast – then
the rest!"

This morning, we started early with a visit to Shannon
(chiropractor friend) – to get ready for surgery. We both went
thru the pre-operative stuff – which had a few moments of
excitement when they couldn't find the "tumour" with the
ultrasound. We had a moment of almost elated false hope.
"We're cured! We're cured!" Finally they causally commented,
"We'd have to do a mastectomy if we couldn't find the spot."

Meanwhile, I retreated to the waiting room. Judith helped get us through the morning. Paul Levy came by and distributed positive vibrations. Now, as the shock waves diminish, Gary Bunch, my 'coach for the day', heads home. Gary is a long standing tradition when we are in crisis. As he left, Rose Galati and her mother arrived with "dinner". We just observed the Marshian version of how to get over "surgery" – spaghetti and meat balls. She just ate her third bowl. Marsha is VERY healthy – she just has a few sick cells. Marsha insists that she is becoming a living "Monty Python" with little bits and pieces of Marsha being lopped off – while she challenges the world: "Keep on coming you coward...."

Our tentative plan is to be in Alaska and Yellowknife – on schedule – departing Feb. 20. We haven't had any "confirmation" from the medical establishment about THEIR plans, but WE are part of this treatment plan, and doing important work is certainly very healing for us. So, we intend to lobby heavily to begin the radiation and/or chemo follow-up in early March, AFTER Alaska and Yellowknife.

Marsha is back making pronouncements, a sure sign of health:

> "Well, now I know I won't live forever, but I'm going to live every day as long as I live – just like everyone else."

My perception (Jack) is relief, since it is only recently that Marsha has begun to notice that she isn't eternal. There is still a lot of tread on her tires...so watch out, world, we're soon to be back on the road.

Dream Catchers and Dolphins

"We are really grateful for the lives we have had – and we wouldn't change that..we've had a great life. Our only wish is that we want more of it. So, we will keep on....and we are counting on all your prayers and wishes and chants...to get us thru' another round, and if necessary another, and another and another."

And we are sending reciprocal wishes back to each of you, your families and friends. We are not in this alone – none of us.

Victoria Pollock is rubbing Marsha's feet. She is dropping off. And so ends a long day.

Jack & Marsha

Marsha Forest & Jack Pearpoint

Three Scars on My Breast

Reaching deep into my heart,
new parts are being born.
I am growing into something new,
an older, wiser, woman.
Not feeling old,
young at heart but
older, wiser, grayer.
My new hair is the symbol.
It is strong healthy thick and white.

I am proud of my scars.
I do not want to hide them.
Three scars on my breasts,
one on my abdomen.
Badges of honour.
Badges of courage.
Constant reminders.
Proud of my survival.

I lost my hair, my appetite, my energy.
They are back.
What joy!
The hair on my legs has returned with a vengeance.
A hairy healthy me emerges again.
But I am not the same.
I am not better, nor worse.

Dream Catchers and Dolphins

I am what I am.

I am more sensitive
less sure,
more vulnerable
less angry,
more humble, tender,
passionate.
More forgiving of me
and the human condition.

In facing fear and death
I am facing life.

I didn't choose this illness.
It is not that easy.
I am surviving for many reasons.
It is not my will alone.
It is where I live, my education,
my skilled surgeons,
an amazing medical team,
a friend and therapist without equal,
a love without bounds,
life work that is life giving,
living in a country where medical care is still a right.

I am still scared.

Marsha Forest & Jack Pearpoint

Tuhoe Creed *

"You have permission to be connected to the world."
my Maori guide advised
"Say what you see.
Be.
That's your job.
Be a gesture of universal energy."

I hungered for that permission to be me.
Hungered for life
and after facing death
and surviving on love
I am finally melting the tumors of the future
by shedding the flesh eating birds of the past.
Birds who pecked joy from my soul
ate out my heart
and forced me to play the role of
perfect little girl child
perfect daughter
perfect wife.

With a knife
the surgeon took tumors from my body and my breasts
Mortality tests.

Dream Catchers and Dolphins

I am now
learning to live the Tuhoe creed.
Laughing and crying and letting the mucous flow.
Letting that bird of prey go.

I start to live into my words and watch the bird of fear
fly off my heart to go where she belongs,
to sing her songs.

I will sing mine.
At fifty-six
it's about time.

I smile.

I am reminded of what I already know.
I seek my own path to green
giving voice to the silent scream
and turning me into a song.

** The Tuhoe are a tribe of the Maori People of Aotearoa
(New Zealand)*

Marsha Forest & Jack Pearpoint

A Teardrop In A Purple Crocus

Today I was walking and chatting quietly with myself.
I had just come from my three month medical check in,
always a scary time
always a humbling time
and on my walk I saw
a tear drop
fall from a purple crocus
just opening for the spring.

I heard music.

I realized deeply and profoundly
that in life there is death
in laughter there are tears
and that nothing,
nothing is certain
except this day.
All else is sheer illusion.
Loss has been a theme these past eight months.
Loss of dear good old friends.
Comrades in work and play.
Gone.
Their spirits remain
but oh how we miss their voices,
their bodies, their brilliance, their shine.

Dream Catchers and Dolphins

I am not the same.
My own boundaries are tighter.
I simply don't have the energy
or desire for the petty or the profane.
Greed and vanity bore me.
I want to only be with the real.
I am grateful for every day
and cherish the clarity
to see the purple crocus
and yellow daffodils
unfold with
their tears and music
which mingle with my own.

Toronto feels safe again for me.
It is where my life was saved.
I walk and talk to the city.
I cry my own very private tears.

I feel rich and enriched.
Sad, glad, mad and different.
I am emotionally drained yet full of new energy.
My body wants to stretch
and so does my mind.
My desk is filled with books to read
My head is filled with poetry to write.

My Toronto family consolidates.
My international family is there.
Jack is there.
Deeper every day.

And all I want is to continue
to make a difference.

Walking in the city today
I saw a teardrop
fall out of the purple crocus.
I heard a melody.
And knew I was alive.

Uncle Whitu Said

Uncle Whitu said,
"You know what you need to do."
Clear wise eyes told me straight from his heart.
"You know. You did it.
And you can do it again."

I trusted my wise Maori guide.
His gentle laughter and creased face have seen it all.
War, death, birth, life.
He has few material goods.
He has wealth in wisdom.
He is my guide from half way around the globe.
I listen.

As I face mortality in the eye.
As I lie in bed sweating
from the panic and fear of sickness and death,
I attempt to find what I need. It is inside me.
I make a little list.

I need rest now,
to be near one key friend.
I need to work, write, travel and fly.
I need little aggravation.

I need to be clear about what I need.
I need time,
much much time.
Time to heal. Time to feel.
Time for comfort and nurture.
That's what I need.

Uncle Whitu,
I am listening.
I am walking through my panic
with you as my guide.
Once again I am breathing new life into my bones
guided by a warrior disguised as a wrinkled old man.
Guided by my whanau,
and the spirit of the children of the mist.

Dream Catchers and Dolphins

Vancouver Rain

I was doing a simple chore.
For some reason
the anger came
with searing pain
in the Vancouver rain.

I feel
red hot as coal
hard as ice
definitely not nice
for under the sad
I discover the mad.

Mad as in anger
fire, rage and pain
holding for dear life
onto my name.

For a mere moment
the sun comes out.
A double rainbow pierces the rain filled sky
And dances and dazzles my eye.
I cry.

Marsha Forest & Jack Pearpoint

I must get rid of this fear
Fear that stops the dance
that kills the joy
that stops the song.

I must rip off the mask
face fear eye to eye
let the judges wig fly
the judge who sentences me to die.
The bird on my heart
is aching
to fly.

It is my choice
to claim my own voice.

The web of fright
the weave of pain is beginning
to be washed away
in the Vancouver rain.
Washed away in the Vancouver rain.

Dreamcatchers and Dolphins

Hi Jack,

I have to smile.....Marsha saying that she intends to live every day to the full from now on. Frightening!!! What does she think she's been doing up to now for God's sake? Both you and Marsha have lived at least six lifetimes already to my knowledge!! I can't see what would even slow her/you down let alone stop her/you...certainly **not** cancer. Just at a time when Marsha is beginning to see that she may not live forever, I was just starting to believe that she would!! Your dream perhaps, but my nightmare! (just joking of course)

Thinking of you lots right now and sending everything that's good, wholesome, fun and humourous.

love Kenn J.

PS. By the way, where are they stashing all those lumps that they have been removing? I'd sure hate to bump into them alone on a dark night!

Marsha Forest & Jack Pearpoint

 Hey Thunder (the louder one) !!!

Thanks for continuing to share with me/us. Your doctor said that you have 'invasive breast cancer'. I'd like to remind you, Thunder, that you also have something else ... tis people, tis people, tis people !!!

Thunder, I really do take your dis-ease seriously, I really do (as I do my own). The invasions and intrusions will come, but we have people prepared to turn them back. As does mine, your cancer also can serve as a blessing. How?

It makes us tender ... and softer ... and humble. I'd like to add Thunder that you have been so much more "open" in this chapter. Your beautiful fear has allowed/forced? you to let "life" in. Life comes from others Thunder.

Your life did not start with you, did it? Your life came from somewhere else. Your healing will too. It is good that you called us (your Village) for support. Yea Thunder, it is so good to see you being so touch-able right now (sharing "real" feelings). And your doctor(s) seem to be good. Always remember, your Village is good too !!!

I think you've also been given the opportunity to learn and teach something else from this chapter, Thunder. Just as MAPS must be "person centered", it should be more than evident to you now that community building (a.k.a. villaging) must be "support centered". Hopefully, we'll learn from this invasion that we should make it a habit of turning to one another whenever possible. Whether we lift off from the "edge" and "fly", or

191

Dream Catchers and Dolphins

whether we lift off and "fall", there should be no doubt that soft hands will always be there for those who are willing to seek them.

Again,
one who's been caught

Shafik

Dearest Thunder

Light, energy, synergy, prayers and laughter we send you.........What surprising news from you. Your strong spirit shines so brightly.

It is amazing that you have been embraced by the native community at just the right time. I too have connections that I gain much strength from. I was gifted a drum (if you remember) and I will play it for you. It sounds likeyou are feeling very connected to spirit animals who live in the water. I will look for something to send to you that evokes that strength. You might like to read anything by Paula Gunn Allen. Here is one of my favourite quotes from *"Messengers of the Wind. Native American Women Tell their Life Stories"*:

"My mother told me stories about cooking and childbearing; she told me stories about gods and heroes, about fairies and elves, about goddesses and spirits; she told me stories about the land and the sky.... She told me European stories and Laguna stories; she told me Catholic stories and Presbyterian stories; she told me city stories and country stories; she told me stories about living and stories about dying. And in all of those stories she told me who I was, who I was supposed to be, whom I came from, and who would follow me. In this way she taught me the meaning of the words she said, and that all life is a circle and everything has a place within it."

Surgery yesterday, a new day today. On the path to wellness and continued work......you are quite a woman. I send you my love, friendship and healing thoughts..........Soon, stay the course........bye for now,

Know you're not alone, you are loved and cared for too. Thanks Jack, talk soon.

Deb K.

Dreamcatchers and Dolphins

 *In reply to a phone conversation with Marsha about being "Out Of Control"*

Dear "arrogant b...." (to use your own words about yourself in our phone call today),

You called ... you said you were "frantic". You said you were "out of control". Yes Thunder, you are out of control. You really don't have control over this (what part of "don't" don't you understand?????). You speak a lot about your fear. Thunder, I don't think "fear" is your main monster (though it is real ... I do know this). I think your biggest monster is "acceptance", or your lack of acceptance of your present reality.

You refuse to accept that you won't be able to "do" all of the things you want to do right now ... and you definitely won't be able to do some things. But you can do a lot of the things you'd like to. Thunder, try not to decide that your "present" medical condition will be your future one as well. I said "try" because this is so hard to do ... real hard to do ... yet necessary to do.

Thunder, if I'm hearing you correctly (and I think that I am), I think you've already decided that you aren't going to get better. I definitely can tell that you certainly "fear" you may not get better. I wish that I could help you think another way. Maybe I will be able to later ... right now I can't.

Finally, you said you don't want to die. Then don't !!! But let me ask you something, "how long do you want to live?". And "how do you want to live?"

Marsha Forest & Jack Pearpoint

Let's discuss this soon, okay? I was told that "people who are prepared to die don't easily die". Try to shift your thinking if you can. Use your music, your friends, your villagers and your medicines (yea, I did say your medicines). I know that "our" medicines don't make us feel good but guess what – if you feel bad, that means that you are still alive because dead things can't feel anything. Take one step at a time Thunder, one step at a time !!!   *And let the mucous flow ...*

Give my love and warmth to Lightning.

Shafik

Dreamcatchers and Dolphins

Febuary 7, 1997

Hi There!

Dear friend Shafik (i.e. big loud Thunder),

First things first. Let's get back to calling me "Thunder" and drop the arrogant "b" term. That was yesterday and today is back to Thunder. OK?

First of all. I will get better because Jack needs me and I need to continue our work 'cause the level of stuff in the world is getting crazier and it needs **all** of us. And you need my calls to challenge your skills as a "healer". I am a challenge.

I saw 'healer Paul' today and we had a great talk and cry; and talked a lot about my talks with you. I had a weird dream the other night and for once I woke up and wrote it down for Jack and Paul. It is very instructive I believe. I was in New York City and I wanted to get to Queens. The cab drivers, two white guys, were taking the wrong route and charging a fortune. They took me to a cousin I don't even like, although she's not awful, and I was feeling trapped. Ending. I got up; got out; and took another cab and lo and behold met Jack in Queens and we continued our journey together. That and the image of the 9 Mexican Turtles who carry all the shit in my body off to a deep reef – where the sharks take away the bad cells leaving me scuba diving with my buddy Jack and the turtles and the dolphins (not the Miami dolfins)...Ha ha. I will get better. Jack will get over this cold. We will be together, all of us, at the summer institute. Watch out world, here comes Thunder and Lightening. And, I will also feel out of control... like shit, like hell and I will call out and reach out to my friends for HELP.

YES, humbly I remain your pal,
Thunder

196

WOW !!! You're Getting It !!!

Peace Thunder,

Your message to me was so beautiful. I love your attempts to "hear" and to "deal" with what your village-mates are saying to you. You're doing good Thunder, better than you think that you are. But it ain't fun, I do know that.

You're dealing with a lot Thunder, a lot more than most people can ever imagine. I'm not talking about your cancer either (many have "been there, done that"). I'm referring to your having to deal (everyday) with the reality of your possible death, and having to think about it because of some medical challenge (as opposed to sudden death). Welcome to the world of so many young African males who also wonder (everyday) if they'll make it through (though their deaths tend to come about suddenly ... by gunshot).

Most of us live with the privilege of hardly ever having to think about our deaths. You don't have this privilege Thunder, nor do you have the right to remain silent. Let's all learn from this !!!

You know what Thunder? A whole ocean can't sink a ship, or even a raft ...unless what? ... Unless it gets inside or onto the ship, or raft. Having become your "grass-roots" therapist, I encourage you to continue to be careful about what you let "into" or "onto" your space. You are already doing this and I really believe you are doing well because of this (only allowing things to be done the way you need them to be done). I'm talking about how you "invited" your supporters in; how you've allowed your doctors and their medicines to play their proper roles, and finally, how you correctly (I believe) ruled other things out such as ... well, you know !!!. This is called, "taking care of one's self". and I think you are. Continue to do so, okay?

Keep flapping your wings Thunder. I know Lightning will too ...

Peace to you both.

Shafik

 **Village-less? Circle-less?**

Thunder, you asked, "What do people do when they lack a village, or circle?".

Yes, I think you're right. Suicide is a commonly made choice. But sometimes people choose to kill somebody else (another option).

Regarding suicide, I believe that when people commit suicide, they are at a point in which their "pain" is sooooooo bad, that the only way they know how to get rid of that pain is to get rid of the "body" (in which that pain is "housed"). So they kill themselves (ie. their pain). I sincerely believe that if we'd be willing to commit to villaging, this could resolve a lot of pain for a lot of people ... tis people, tis people, tis people.

Someone once wrote, "In a cold, cold world, you need some friends to keep you warm". When I feel scared, or "not very good", I don't take two pills and then call my doctor in the morning. I first call two friends, and then (more often than not) I usually don't need a doctor (ask Shina, or Bahiya ... my two best friends). This is learned behaviour because I (like most people) was taught to "go it alone".

But despite all that's been said so far, being without a village (or community) results in what I believe to be the worse (yet preventable) disease of all – **loneliness**. Villaging is hard. But I don't concentrate on the hard part. Villaging is necessary; and its necessity is the part I concentrate on. So in

Dream Catchers and Dolphins

your spare time (of course you have a lot of this, don't you?), build a village or two, ... or three. We must allow no one to be village-less. Will share more on this later.

one who builds villages,

Shafik

Re: Thanks For Support???

Hey Thunder ...

You're welcome. I don't know another way to
be except supportive ... I was raised "village-style".
Those blood drains (tubes) are yukky aren't they? Shina's
were removed about two weeks ago. A weird feeling when
they're being pulled out, huh?

"Hi" Lightening (ok, I'll use the correct spelling ... y'all
don't like Shafikabonics?).
So Lightening, are you having fun yet?
Remember, this too shall pass.

Yesterday (Friday) my doctor told me, maybe "warned" me,
to increase my medicines. I decided (afterwards) that I will
stop all medicines for a few weeks just so that I can get a little
stronger, then I'll "do" them again.

He said that I'm in "stroke" zone with my blood pressure
being so high. Well, I've been here before, I'm not sweating it.
It already returned almost to normal today.

I love my doctor ... he's tolerated me for 18 years now. I
got rid of my doctors that preceded him (my first two years). I
finally feel good today. I was starting to get scared, and
discouraged. It seemed like I was gonna always be that way
(not feeling quite like myself, dizzy at night etc).

Dealing with Thunder's stuff helped me a lot. It reminded
me of what "I already know", that we must take it just one day

at a time. Deep huh? If you think that sharing this with Thunder might be useful, please do so (if she hasn't read it already).

Peace be yours Lightening ... hope you're feeling a little better.

One who's been caught !!!

Shafik

February 7, 1997

The Fire is Dancing!

Dearest friends,

I am home and I just made a fire and it is dancing. The '*Canyon Trilogy*' of Carlos Nikai is playing on the tape recorder and I am lying cosy and warm under the amazing Star blanket presented to us by our Aboriginal friends in Winnipeg. Jack has just gone out to get some cough medicine for himself and to get a breath of fresh Toronto air (perhaps that's an oxymoron in any city.) The home care nurse, Anne, has just been here to change my dressings and drain my drains. She wanted to give me pain killers to do my exercises for range of motion in my arm, but I assured her I was not in pain (at least physical), and we did the exercises and I did just fine. Hopefully the drain will come out in two more days. We gave her a copy of *Inclusion News* and sent her on her way.

The physical side of this drama is not the main difficulty. It is the **mind** side. The fear and terror comes at me now and then, like a massive tidal wave. When it comes, it is good to have a listening heart nearby to feel the tears and fears and share the scared shitless parts. Jack is that friend.

And you out there are also all the listening hearts. But this is reciprocal, so feel free to ask for anything back that you might need. If we can do it, we will.

What I find incredibly difficult now is to find the balance between the need for solitude and the need for people. The energy needed for phone calls and company is draining. Except for a few people, I am staying off the phone for a few days. Usually I love the phone. But now I can't make arrangements, nothing is for sure, everything is in limbo...I am waiting. I hate waiting, even in the best of times. I am not the most "waiting" kind of person. But this is out of my hands. The doctors say come back to the hospital and hear the test results on Thursday, Feb. 13. We will go. Till then – we wait. That is the 'crazy making' part of this situation. So I have made a sanity plan that involves reading, movies, solitude and music during the day – and writing. E-mail is a wonderful way I can keep in touch; still be connected and yet not have the drain of energy that the telephone absorbs. Reading your notes is an amazing way to be connected and linked. It is like a melody.

I definitely want to write something about this experience. I feel it might actually help others. A voice in me says, "write", so I will. I'll use the e-mail I've been sending as a start to a small book on how to survive any life crisis.

The message, for me, is that while we are waiting and working to create a society where medical care will be truly caring and available to all (and where that is a RIGHT) what the hell do we do in the middle of cutbacks, etc.?

I have received great physical care. My surgeon is brilliant and skilled. I cannot expect him also to be sweet and caring. So, if I spent all my time being mad at everyone I'd really be sick. Yes, I will be at health care demos to save medicare in Canada and I will get more active on that front.

In the meantime, I will build the "village" that Shafik keeps reminding me that will be my healing team.

Some incredible vignettes of this journey at the hospital:

← Paul Levy our therapist and friend made time to come to the hospital to just say hello to Jack while I was in surgery.

← Judith was there and quietly read.

← Gary Bunch was by Jack's side.

← At dinner (no one expected me to eat) the one and only Rose appeared with her magic spaghetti and I demolished 3 servings much to the amazement of all the nurses

← Then Victoria emerged with a beautiful plant and a pink Teddy Bear, we now call L'Chaim (to life). She sat and massaged my feet while Jack went home to get some sleep.

The Rose Quartz Circle is in Action.

I didn't sleep one wink at the hospital. I was wired. I had survived surgery. I was also terrified of what comes next – so I watched TV all night. Thanks to channel 40, the Bolshoi Ballet did a very long ballet I had never seen, The Stone Flower. It was incredibly beautiful.

When my surgeon came to inspect me the next morning I was sitting dressed in real clothes and Jack and I were reading all the e-mail. He said if I promised to rest, I could go home! Shannon, the miraculous friend and chiropractor, appeared.

She came home with us and treated my body and central nervous system; and lo and behold, I slept for the next many hours and when I awoke I finished the last of the Rose spaghetti and then went back to sleep.

Jack is exhausted and has a pretty bad coughing cold (big surprise) so we made him stay in bed last night and this morning. I am serving dinner in bed. We're watching junk TV tonight.

The next big day of this war against cancer (and believe me

that's what it is) is the two appointments next Thursday Feb. 13 with the surgeon and the oncologist. We will then know a bit more and start the treatment plan of action. I am of course terrified of radiation and chemo *again*. But I did it once and I can and will do it again because I love life and it is worth every attempt at preserving it. But have no illusions, the thought of it all sends me into those cataclysms of terror.

In other words I will do what I can do. That's really all I can do. Trust us. We are doing everything possible and everything that is right for us.

The most important lesson here is that each family must truly find their own PATH. What is good for us may be awful for someone else. The real listeners hear what you are really saying and help you along that PATH. John O and Shafik have been masters at this.

I appreciate all your e-mails and today we got our very first virtual flower bouquet from a friend in Winnipeg. WOW! That was terrific.

I must share (with all of you) some more of Shafik's amazing words to me. He has been through all this and so has his beautiful partner and wife, Shina. He writes, "Thanks for continuing to share with us. Your doctor said you have invasive breast cancer. I want to remind you, Thunder, that you also have something else...tis people, tis people, tis people!!!"

He continues, "The cancer can also make us more humble, tender and softer. Your beautiful fear has allowed/forced you to let "life" in. Life comes from others Thunder. Your life didn't start with you now did it? Your life came from somewhere else and your healing will too. It is good that you called us, your village, for support. Yeah Thunder. Your doctors seem real good and always remember your Village is real good too!!!"

"I think we've all been given the opportunity to learn something else too. Just as MAPS and PATH are person centered, they are really SUPPORT centered. Hopefully we will all learn from this invasion that we must make it a habit of turning to one another whenever possible. Whether we lift off from the edge and fly, or whether we lift off and fall, there is no doubt that soft hands will always be there for those who are willing to seek them. This I write as one who has been caught many times...."(Shafik)

As I sit here with my beautiful fire dancing, I also want to make sure that if these messages make anyone uncomfortable let us know and we won't send them. I've really learned that too lately. I am not telling anyone to do remotely what I am doing. I am sharing my route and it seems to be helping and inspiring others who are dealing with a variety of other human life crisis – divorce, depression, losing a job, problems with kids, etc.

The work continues. The office is open and operating. Cathy is here each evening. Orders are going out and we are operating as best we can.

I am sure of only one thing – loneliness kills. Without Jack I would surely go under. But two is not enough. It surely does take a whole village to raise a child. A network doesn't simply form in a crisis. This network has shared the celebrations, the struggles, the ups and the downs. There are new friends out there, but there are also many of us that have been connected for almost 20 years. May we continue...

One more thought. In the book by Paul Pearsall, *Superimmunity,* he has a definition of health I really like. He says, "Health is the ability to survive illness. It is not the absence of illness that defines health, it is the ability of the body to fight back."

I really like this. The people I am avoiding, like the plague, are people into the sick model. Anyone who treats me like I am sick I run away from. Granted I am struggling with a major and potentially life threatening cell disease, but I see myself as healthy and refuse to be treated like anything but a healthy person. All the people, who don't understand that our work makes me strong and that travel is a joy for us, are totally missing the point. I will rest, yes, but the purpose of resting and solitude is to get healthy and strong enough to work again. It is a balancing act.

Please recommend great books and films. Our favourites at the moment in film are *Shine* and *The English Patient*. The book *The English Patient* is also amazing. For a laugh, I am reading (so I can educate Cathy into great Jewish expressions) a book called *"Every Goy's Guide to Common Jewish Expressions"* by Arthur Naiman (also recommended for Jews who don't know their *punim* from their *pupik*.) If you don't know what punim and pupik are ask or figure it out.

OK. Time for dinner. Very much love and very many thanks for all your thoughts and wishes.

Marsha and coughing Jack

Bravo!!!

I am assuming that "bravo" has something to do with the word "brave". If so, I feel it is an entirely appropriate accolade to pass on to the two of you – given what you continue to endure, and find a way to thrive through (temporary flu ruses aside).

It is true that "the book" is one of inspiration, and the gifts, talents, network and capacity that the two of you have would seem to indicate that you are positioned to share a story that many others would hold in a much smaller circle. If encouragement is needed, then I join the body of encouragement.

Relief, pride, gratefulness and humility emanate from our home to yours this evening. Send e-mail from Alaska.

When you feel your breath returning along with the colour in your cheeks, let me know if there is a time to drop by and say hello.

Dave Hasbury

Dreamcatchers and Dolphins

Dear Marsha,

You're words and feelings of insight are wonderful! And you are most definitely a "gentle warrior". I have started dubbing a collective of friends, such as you, (that are warriors from the feminine perspective) as "No Shit Chicks". This is a high honour.

You are most definitely a NO SHIT CHICK. A No Shit Chick is a woman who, when a major challenge is presented, doesn't say, "Why me?" and then wallows. We say "Why me?" And realize "why not me?" We have strength, have spiritual "connectedness", have community, and have a vision for ourselves, life, and the moment. We will get past the hurdles, no matter how scary, challenging, etc.

That doesn't mean we aren't vulnerable, freaked out and confused. But we allow the emotions to come through us, not become totally of us.

I had a lump removed from my breast in the fall. After the ovarian thing (which we both know all too well) I was beginning to think I was destined to have a body that looked like a road map and lose pieces bit by bit. But I also realized that road maps take you somewhere. And I've sure been blessed with an unusual journey so far.

My surgeon was wonderful and kind. He also has a daughter with MS wasting away in a Brazilian prison. So I guess his own pain and fear have led him to his own amazing personal road map. We vets of life's skirmishes may be a bit battered and bruised, but are we ever privy to some amazing experiences! (easy for me to stay at the hind end of one such experience, right?)

I know I'm not ever going to be "out of the woods". Or so the "experts" say. But I also know the whole time here is a crap shoot for everyone, regardless of health and any other obstacles. We're all incredibly vulnerable, no exceptions.

Those of us that have had fate touch us on the shoulder (to remind us of that vulnerability) are now part of the great cosmic "inside joke". So we may as well enjoy the ride for whatever time we will be present for it. I don't want to miss a moment or overlook an opportunity. This desire comes from a place of excitement and loving awe, not fear and desperation.

Anyway, just the perspectives of a west coaster. They do say the country is tilted and the nuts roll to the west, so who knows.....

Thanks for the tidbit about the book re: Jewish sayings. I've been noticing just how many sayings I had picked up from my grandmother, and assumed everyone understands. Now I can look to something to help them translate!

Get well gently!

Much love and many many thoughts and prayers for your progress,

Linda P.

Dreamcatchers and Dolphins

Hi Marsha & Jack,

I am one of those "new friends" who was touched by your positive spirit and amazing commitment during a PATH workshop in Nelson, B.C. I have been checking for your messages every day and sharing them with the rest of the Cranbrook crew (South East B.C.) that also attended your Nelson workshop.

I have wanted to connect but was hesitant – "They don't really know who I am". "What do I say?". "They're already hearing from everyone they want to hear from!", etc., etc. etc.

I realized all along that they were excuses – avoidances. Maybe out of fear, maybe out of lack of trust.......but today I realized (or remembered) that the more difficult it is to do, the more important it is to do it!!

Marsha, I continue to be amazed at your determined spirit to "fight this thing". That makes sense and I couldn't imagine you doing it any other way. It is your determination that others learn from. This sharing it and telling it are tools to help many others face their "demons" also. I am going to confess (as I tune in to what is really happening for me) that I feel intimidated by you – it is part of why I haven't written. It is a culmination of many things but the basis is my lack of self assurance. Someone of your strength (and I say that in the sense of your spirit, your conviction and your presence) stirs up my self doubts.

I, along with many others, strongly believe that you have the strength, the knowledge (within) and the power to fight this battle and win. I want you to know that you are constantly in my thoughts and I too send you much healing energy and love. I think your sharing has stirred up many emotions for people and I also know that your openness is a great gift in opening hearts, and fears, so we (the outside circle) can search a little deeper and hopefully be a little more aware as we continue on our journey.

Graham, your Cranbrook connection, also sends his love – he was deeply affected by your first e-mail and you may have already heard from him. The rest of the Cranbrook crew send love and best wishes.

Thank you for allowing me to share with you, and especially thank you for stirring up old doubts so I can finally work through them and let them go!!

Hello and love to Jack as he shares this part of the journey with you. Without knowing either of you that well, it is obvious that your love for each other is very strong and his being there makes all the difference.

Keep challenging the fears and the "monsters". Keep smiling and laughing. Keep sharing and receiving. You continue to be in my thoughts!

Beth C.

Dreamcatchers and Dolphins

Dear Marsha:

It pleases me so to read that you are deciding what is right for you. Doing what you can do, engaging in a waiting plan and resting for the purpose of returning to the road. Don't think for a minute that I don't recognize that your work is lifework and in moving from minute to minute each day, you are doing your work, and being your work, and all of that which you already know! Lifework! I must thank you for including me in the details...as you share what you learn, I learn, too. Here is a strange and somewhat uncomfortable thought that I am learning from your engagement with cancer. I don't know how that thought will rest with you, and please send it on its way or make a place for it, as you wish. As I got the first message from you on "support needed", I realized that this would be a reciprocal thing. Not that I necessarily wanted it that way...I just knew that's how it WAS. I am a little reluctant to know it, but it makes it less scary that you know it, too.

Tomorrow is Mardi Gras in my beloved New Orleans. I urge you to revel in any way that strikes you! Et toi, la bas!! Laissez les bon temps roulez! At Inclusion Works, we are preparing for the conference in El Paso this Thursday-Saturday. You will be in our midst; we will be 1600 strong, and we will speak your name, remembering that you choose life, today, on Thursday, and for the foreseeable future.

Still dancing in solidarity with you and your choice to live,

Charlene C-G

Marsha,

Well, I'm in my nest (my "pigeon whole" – a quote from an early article I wrote said we wouldn't pigeon hole if we saw the pigeon whole) for almost thirty six hours. Either Joe or wonder niece Erin has kept me up to date with your messages. You both are such talented people ... you make words into crayons and then draw pictures!

Today I am going to go to Vespers at the monastery near here. No, I'm not Catholic but I don't think you have to be in order to feel the presence of prayer and peace there. At five o'clock the monks will begin to chant. The sound of their music lifts and swirls into the smoke from the incense and then drifts slowly down and settles like a warm blanket around our feet. Going there I realized for the first time that prayer doesn't lift into the sky, borne on angel wings to God's ear. Prayer does something different. It envelops the prayer and the prayed for, as if heaven exists somewhere between the two. Today I am going to Vespers and today I pray that Thursday comes quickly. I will pray that Marsha and Jack survive the wait by gathering strength for the next part of the journey.

On another note, I just finished a new article wherein I had a very Marsha inspired line that reads:
"Unfortunately the parents didn't realize that the phrase 'in the best interests of the child' is educational spin doctoring for the more direct 'get that fucking brat out of my classroom.'"
I wrote that and chuckled and chuckled and chuckled. Joe came and read it over my shoulder and laughed saying, 'That's a good line.' I told him I was laughing because the first time I

ever heard Marsha speak, she showed me what it was to be uncompromising – but with grace and wit. I remember someone in the audience standing up and saying in a conspiratorial tone, "Now, Marsha, you must admit that some children shouldn't be allowed in the classroom." Marsha, I don't know if you remember this. You stood, looked thoughtful and said, "Well, I will admit something." The woman nodded and smiled wisely. You then said, "Yes, (pause for dramatic effect) I will admit that some teachers shouldn't ever be allowed in a classroom." Cheers and laughter from the audience. Point made! Even the woman who asked laughed!! I was so impressed. If you can make them laugh, you can make them think, I thought to myself.

Well, enough of this you must get tired of my blather from Quebec so ... tonight at five prepare to receive blessings from St. Benoit du lac!!

Dave Hingsburger

Marsha Forest & Jack Pearpoint

Dear *whanau,*

    I've been "disconnected" too long. Last week with uncle Joe in hospital, very ill but now recovered. Then on Waitangi Day, which was holidays, I was up in Hamilton sharing the thesis with those who had contributed so far – it went well. Then away for a *hui* in Rotorua for the weekend. Only returned today to the most time wasting meeting!! Things are just hotting up on the Maori political front and I feel drained already with all the negativity!!

    Anyway despite this you were never far from my thoughts, Uncle Whitu as well, with a.m & p.m. prayers. We were on the phone last night and he wanted an update; and when asked for some words of wisdom – he just said "she knows her task in life is to keep bringing people together – the *whanau* of the world need her". So he just confirms what you really already know. Myself, I'm just plain selfish and want my sister around to "boss around", to write wonderful poetry, to cook wonderful meals, to take our moko Kura with the Toronto mokos for adventures (open them up to greater possibilities), to soak longer in her bubble bath.

    I ache inside thinking of the bad times you go through. I get mad too; and then think positive, and remember the wise words of brother Shafik and send those through mother earth.

    I miss you all and will be back for a longer chat. I'm so pleased Barbara is with you – real whanau you two!!
Love you,
Te Ripowai

217

Dreamcatchers and Dolphins

 Dear Marsha (and Jack),

I appreciate your taking the time to send this email. It means a lot to me. I am glad to know that my feeble attempts (and so they feel) at expressing some feelings, thoughts, sense of the Spirit (to you) come through underneath the fumbling words.

(As you requested,) I will try to think about themes that I might hear emerging. I just have this image (of you) emerging out this enormous circle and all of us holding hands around you. You are going through just ONE of the many things we all fear. Your struggling to reach out and having the courage to share your terror and tears, your joy and hope and downright 'orneriness' (my Texas background comes out more the older I get) provides such a sense of hope. Maybe, just MAYBE, in similar circumstances each of us may experience a circle of friends too; not to take away the terror, but to share it.

And finally for NOW. You know years ago, in a spiritual time for my wife and I, we sought 'tongues' of the Spirit – utterances of language and song. Periodically they come as I struggle and hope and work. And I think of this now and find a song of peace rising to you Marsha. And to us All.

> Gentle on the wind
> She rides the storm!!
> The thunder claps!
> The warm wind blows overhead and all around
> And on the hill. . . she stands.
> Arms to the sky
> Eyes twinkling bright and a face of dazzled joy!

Marsha Forest & Jack Pearpoint

And to the rumbling foes
She lifts her clasped hands together in firm defiance.
BEGONE OH DARKNESS
AND COME NO MORE!
She shouts and the words echo the valleys
of the world around.

And like a ripple in a pond
The silence spreads
The light circles on the edge, a spark, an ember
And blazing into glory the Dawn comes
Exploding in ever-raptured colors of blue and green
and amber glowing.

And in the east
The smallest of creatures lifts Her voice
So small
So small
So small.

And on the hill they finally come
Concentric circles
Holding hands and holding hands and singing,
shouting
A raucous melody of joy building and floating and
shining forth in melody.

And she falls to her knees
In pain
And joy
And hope.

Dream Catchers and Dolphins

And so these words came Marsha.

In love,

Your friend and seeking community builder.

Michael P.

Marsha Forest & Jack Pearpoint

Marsh and Jack

Needless to say, thoughts of you weigh heavy on my mind and in my heart. I surround you with love, tranquility, health and peace on this day and impatiently await your next correspondence.

I remember all too well, when I lost my family, how folks in my "circle" would comment on my strength; and I remember how that would elicit an anger from deep within. No one, I felt, could possibly say that if they knew the fear, sorrow and pain I was feeling. But I am able to look back on that period of my life and realize that indeed, I had tremendous strength. Some that came from within, and even more that came from the support of those around me.

You both have so much strength and have already won so many battles. Now the battle has become a war. And you are not alone. You have troops from around the globe that are fighting with you, side by side. Use us. Use the strength of the love and healing energy that surrounds you and you will conquer.

I love you both.

Melissa M.

Dreamcatchers and Dolphins

February 7, 1997

Life!

Dear John,

I seem to feel better if I can vent – so here goes. Jack is in bed with a real doozey of a cold/flu but he is now on antibiotics and can breathe better already. He deserves a cold. I am feeling totally overwhelmed and exhausted. This waiting and being at the mercy of everyone and having to be so nice is really hard. Visiting nurses have to come everyday to check the drain and dressings. You never know when they are coming so you can't make any plans. No control again. And every time I think about going back to the doctors (on Thursday) I go into a cold sweat.

Jack and I are doing great. As long as I don't blame myself and genuinely cry from fear and sadness, he is fine. The divorce papers only come out when I do the apologizing stuff, so I am not doing that. I cry a lot but it is healthy crying and I am giving Jack lots of room to feel awful too.

We plan to get on that plane for Alaska and Yellowknife. The hope is alive and well. We did go to Winnipeg so there is hope for the North too.

Then I know treatments of some kind will start and I will deal with that as it comes.

I am truly up and down. What else could I be? I wish there was a formula to deal with this. "Write your own script," they say. Well I sure didn't choose this movie to play in. All I can do is the best I can do. I sure understand why some people give up. Without Jack I would. Love really is the answer. It can come from a child, or a lover, or a parent, but it has to come from somewhere or we are sunk.

I think you hit an important point when you said that Josie's "advice" was universal truth. Like if you jump off a tall building you ain't gonna fly, you are going to break your neck. Even if you wish you'd fly you won't. So I wish I didn't have all this going on now, I'd prefer to be not in this situation but I am in it and I can even now be thankful for my life, for Jack and for friends like you.

When you said that I was never far from your thoughts, it really touched me. It makes me cry. Knowing how much Jack cares and friends care is a great solace and healer.

OK. Time for my mystery book again. Thanks for being out there.

This writing is an essential part of my keeping my immune system strong. I have to have an outlet for the fear. So I have various levels of e-mail. It is like the circles. There's the totally uncensored stuff to a very few and then the broader thoughts shared with the many.

A friend brought a beautiful tray of Sushi. Time to eat it.

Stay in touch. Love to Connie.

Marsha and 'coughing' Jack

Dreamcatchers and Dolphins

February 12, 1997

Dream Catcher...

Dear friends,

These past two days have not been easy. The waiting till Thursday for the doctor appointments is difficult (to put it mildly). I think to myself, how does a parent watch a sick child and wait for a diagnosis? How do we glibly tell parents that their child will NEVER walk, talk, learn...

How do people then go home and survive? The answer is that many don't. Those who do, as we are so personally learning, have the support to say, "Hell no, you don't know." Judith Snow's parents said that. Norman Kunc's mom said that. Many of you reading this have said that.

The power of this circle is intense. I am overwhelmed by the passion, the beauty and the depth of the letters, faxes and gifts we continue to receive. Today a package arrived. Jack is in bed with the flu. He is exhausted, physically and mentally. I was working with a young health practitioner to make sure her practice is one of love and caring. The bell rang. A huge package arrived from the North West Territories. It was packed with such care; and as layer after layer of paper came off we recognized the shape of a large dreamcatcher.

The paper peeled off to reveal a rose wood braided dreamcatcher designed and made for us by our dear friends in Yellowknife. The story will unfold as they send us what they asked the artist to weave into the dreamcatcher. It is magical and will greet everyone who enters our home.

The magic however is in the weaving of the circle around each and every one of us. The circles are like ripples in a still lake. It seems my message is going out to others and yes you have my full blessing to share these musings with whosoever you wish.

An important person in my life has been TeRipowai's, (and now my) Uncle Whitu; a wise and wrinkly elder of the Tuhoe tribe. Uncle Whitu usually gives me one line of wisdom in our hours together. We share laughs and food and when I am ready he will give me what we call "my line." The first year we met him, as we were leaving, he just looked at Jack and me and said, "Now it is time for you to go home. Simply say what you see." And we did. And we made our "*WHAT DO YOU SEE SLIDE SHOW*" that has meant so much to many people who see it...

Te Ripowai spoke to Uncle Whitu the other night. She said, "Marsha wants some words of wisdom." I could see him laughing at that. Uncle Whitu is the real thing. He doesn't take himself, me, or this wisdom stuff too seriously – except in the broadest and best sense of the word. He told Te Ripowai to tell me, "She knows her task in life is to keep bringing people together – the whanau (families) of the world need her." I cried.

When we left New Zealand, Jack was given a token that he wears around his neck. His token means "binder of people". The message is the same and we hear it. As far as Uncle Whitu is concerned, just continue working to serve people. *Tis people, tis people, tis people.*

This e-mail is binding a network together. My words, like

yours, are coming straight from the heart. I thought today I shouldn't, or wouldn't, write again 'till I have more information. Then I realized that these words are pouring out of me for a reason. It is my way to survive the waiting. I am reaching out to "speak the fear and do it anyway," (it is life). It is my book. I am tired of judging what I write. It is as it is; and the words seem to be helping me and reaching many other hearts. So be it.

Te Ripowai went on to say that she selfishly wants me around so she can boss me around as sisters do with one another. The messages are real, earthy and from the souls of my friends. And Te Ripowai, I will boss you back too... And we shall take the Toronto Mokos and Aotearoa Moko on many adventures. *(Mokos* are grandchildren).

Jack is still feeling lousy from the flu and he has been sleeping for a few days. This I think is an excellent response to this week. Cathy keeps us all on our toes and the office is functioning well. Physically, I feel fine, but I am waging a mental battle against fear and uncertainty. This is real. My will to survive is fierce. I will do what it takes! Most of all I need Jack by my side and all the incredible energy around us. Jack can taste my tears when they speak of fear and uncertainty – he only wants to kill me when I do the "I am ruining your life" speech or the "did I do something wrong" speech. So I don't do it. I just cry from my heart and then we can hold each other and get on with life.

In the midst of some blueness and my yucky mood yesterday, the bell rings and another largish and a smallish package arrive. Both were wonderful. Gerv and Sue had sent us our favourite show music that we love to listen to in England. And Susan

Young sent the prize winner for laughter – "TICKLE ME ELMO". Elmo is a red weird looking doll thing that when you pat his tummy once, he laughs; twice he laughs harder; and the third time he literally vibrates. We cracked up totally. Elmo is sitting here now and shares a laugh with all of you, for if we lose the ability to laugh, we will really be finished. We are no where near finished – so we laugh with Elmo.

As we wait for Thursday, we thank you all for your thoughts. For Valentine Day, I want to give thanks to the power of the circle. All we can wish for you is that your circles are full – be it hundreds of people or a few. The universal message is truly the Maori proverb that I thought was ancient but was made up by Te Ripowai, my friend and baby sister...she said, "Laugh and cry and let the mucus flow." (and we are.)

I am about to make wonderful spaghetti with a gorgeous sauce made by Rose Galati, another sister of the heart. Everyone is being very respectful of our private space and need for solitude, and at the same time being there for us. It is all a balancing act right now - the need for space, solitude and people. The right people are here as they have been for years. The e-mail people are beautiful. In all this, the lesson is that none of us can do it alone, or has to do it alone.

People are there in any community. In a time of tragic economic cutbacks, it is truly not safe to be alone. The time to build the circle is when you are strong and well. We will all have times of crisis. It is part of life. But the danger now is that we simply call (on) the circle, and not demand that the government provide the best care for all its citizens. So we fight on two fronts – the political and the personal. One is not enough. Both are necessary.

So thanks for the poetry, the music, the love and the laughter. This will be a book. Title suggestions welcome.

We made it through another day – we worked, we laughed (thanks to Elmo), we cried. And now we will watch a video; and eat spaghetti; and as Uncle Whitu advises, we will continue to weave the community into something new – a community of caring and sharing.

Ah yes, thanks to Dr. Harry McCoy. Harry and Kaye McCoy are friends we met through Anne Malatchi in Virginia. Harry is a medical oncologist. He has given us the knowledge, and more than that, the hope that treatment is possible. He cares. He and Kate (also a doctor) called us Sunday night. I didn't want to bother them. Can you believ it, they called us... This caring is what I find so lacking in the regular medical stuff. I am soooo fortunate to have it in Paul and in Shannon and in Harry and Kate, and more.

In the circle, make sure you not only have loving people, but people who can also do things like shop, make the best spaghetti sauce on earth, do a budget, etc.

Enough, enough.
I love you all and I mean it.

Hugs from Marsha and Jack

Marsha

Last night we were driving home from Montreal. I had landed at a decent hour and was hoping to get home early, but the weather Gods conspired against me. The road was treacherous, black ice lurked everywhere, snow blew in huge gusts and blinded us with an odd combination of light and dark. Even though we knew the way home we felt lost and moments grew longer and longer. Joe remarked, 'Isn't it odd that the only thing that keeps us on track is a sense of direction.'

I thought immediately of you; and what you faced today. The hardest thing about your week was that you were on a road, with dangers everywhere, but without knowing the destination of the journey. Remember, whatever the results are, knowing where you are going is half the battle. Fear can settle into resolve. Anxiety can turn into determination. Dread can be a fire that rages against night, rather than a thing that consumes thought.

Well, new friend and old acquaintance, I await news with hopeful prayer.

Dave Hingsburger

Dreamcatchers and Dolphins

 Jack and Marsh,

How wonderful to absorb your hope! And, I share your fear and terror for what might await you tomorrow as you meet with the doctors. I tell you that I am here in your circle – to catch, boost, support, cook, clean, play, laugh, cry – whatever it takes. Thank you for sharing your fears today. Waiting is so hard and I guess until you have done it you just don't know the fear and foreboding. I hate it, but we can't escape it either.

Tomorrow I will be wearing my rose quartz for you both. I pray that the information from the doctors tomorrow will be good. You are strong; and we are here for you. The village surrounds you; and we love you. There is no doubt that Shafik properly named you two Thunder and Lightening. Tell Jack that I hope he is well soon. Also, I think that sleeping for days is a blessing of the spirits to help us through a time in which our minds and bodies need great support and nurturing.

Do you realize that our friendship began back in 1992, when I made my first journey to Montreal? A connection which spanned thousands of miles and millions of possibilities. Though we have not seen each other since February 14, 1995 I feel as if it was yesterday. Remember the wonderful Italian meal we had at the Oakbrook McDonald's center? Flowers and all!!! Let us toast each other on this upcoming Valentine's Day. I agree that what you two will always do best is bond people together. MAY LIFE BE YOURS FOR A VERY LONG TIME!!!!

I LOVE YOU BOTH,
Connie P.

Marsha Forest & Jack Pearpoint

February 13, 1997

Alaska Here We Come...
Guardedly Optimistic!!!

Freeze it – Then Sear it – Two More Weeks

WE just got the best Valentine's Day Gift – more time to work and be together. Thanks for helping us get another extension! And don't stop. We ain't done yet!

We're back from the doctors. We're alive for a while yet. So watch out! The Breast Cancer is **contained** and **treatable**! Radiation will start later in March. The Ovarian Cancer is still in hiding... and although we don't know for sure... we're not packing it in yet! We are "guardedly optimistic!" We want to cheer because the breast cancer results are as good as they can be (given that we have cancer), but we are scared to cheer because the ovarian shadow remains... and may be there for decades...or not. We feel a little like the famous Woody Allen scene when he emerges from the doctor having discovered that he is not terminally ill, and immediately has a crashing depression: "I'm going to live! I'm going to live!...Oh no.. that means I'm going to die! I'm going to die!" Such is life.

We are trying to balance the up and down – so we can get back to work.

This has been a hard week of waiting – and 7 hours of waiting today. My synopsis is that it has been a MAJOR inconvenience. This was NOT in our plan. We had just got "ovarian" worked into our schedule when another little lump halts the parade. But the parade is back on schedule – with some adjustments.

So far the score card is:

Marsha & Jack	vs.	Breast Cancer
3		**0**
Marsha & Jack	vs.	Ovarian Cancer
1		**0**

The good news is we're here for the next round...and hopefully quite a few more. The hard news is that "we don't know" line – which is hard to hear and difficult to live with initially. In time, we will get more comfortable with the uncertainty we all live with. None of us knows the future. It's just that ours is dangling in front of us more dramatically. So, we have work to do to get ready for Alaska and Yellowknife.

Our survival/recovery has only been possible because of an amazing network of friends and supporters. It has been remarkable printing out the e-mail – now three inches thick. The messages, the words, thoughts, prayers, gifts. It has been a "force". It will be a great book. You are all encouraged to hound Marsha on this one. It is **her** book – and this time, it must NOT be set to one side. It needs to get out to the world – now!! Order your book now – suggest titles. Keep the heat on Marsha to write that book.

Are we out of the woods?? No. The fact is we never will be. But we just came out of another "treacherous tangle", and we wouldn't be here without all your support. We trust that we will be able to reciprocate with many of you personally, hopefully in less stressful circumstances. However, you can count on our commitment to do the best work we can, for however long we have, so that the tools and training are shared with as many families and networks as we can. That is our commitment to repay your efforts that have been so critical in getting us through this battle.

We really do hope that we never have to recruit your energy again for this... but if we need your help – we know you will come. You already have. Thank you from the bottom of our hearts.

And now...watch out Alaska and Yellowknife.

Please keep up the chants, prayers and good wishes. It works - and we are more than willing to share it around.

HAPPY VALENTINE'S DAY to one and all!!!

```
      ,d88b..d88b,
      88888888888
      'Y8888888Y'
       'Y8888Y'
        'Y"Y'
         'Y'
```

More from Marsha later......

She has had a bath...(first real one since surgery) and is now a little tuckered...

Jack
(formerly coughing – now just breathing deeply – and finally

out of bed). My flu was really just a massive ruse – to convince Marsha that I couldn't get along without her. It worked!

For those of you who are interested in the medical details (seven hours of waiting was tense!):

Post Operative Report:

Results:
Breast Cancer: -
- Malignant T1 tumour - 1 cm (invasive) – removed
- additional margin removed – clear
- 18 lymph nodes removed – clear (pathology report)

Prognosis - Excellent (given the downer of actually having cancer).

Treatment - 4 weeks of radiation starting in March..

Other related tests:
- bone scan - normal
- CA125 (tumour marker study) – to be determined
- Ultra Sound – "shadow" discovered.. therefore on to...
- CT Scan – shadow near spleen - unconfirmed cause – further monitoring required. This could be post operative scar from the original ovarian surgery – or many other things.

Plan of action ...
First:
← GO to Alaska and Yellowknife
← Return for more "monitoring and/or tests"
← One pathology test (er & pr receptors???) still to come....

THEN.. treatment plan:
← Minimum - one month of daily radiation
← Plus?? Chemo?????
← Another CT scan??? (monitor shadow)

Hope: Continuing Excellent Health while living with a genetically induced disease. (Marsha has Ashkenazim (Jews from Eastern Europe) genes which unfortunately have a high incidence of both breast and ovarian cancer with the other pattern of higher that average survival given the disease.)

Jack

Dream Catchers and Dolphins

Dreamcatchers,

for what it is worth happy valentine's day!!!
you must know that you are loved
friends and family that make the circle
and the circle only grows

> and, no, you should not wait "for news"
> before sharing with the circle
> the news will come
> but the circle is here, now,
> and when all is said and done
> now is all we have
> all we ever get
> all we ever need
> a simple lesson
> that few learn

> use the dreamcatcher well
> that is powerful magic
> and it will help you greatly
> filtering out the crap
> allowing only good to enter

> enjoy this day
> for it is meant for lovers

> give Jack a hug and a kiss for me
> and one for you, too

> *mark p.*

236

Dear Marsha and Jack,

Oh the precious gift of time!! Your news made my heart sing. One day at a time...good news...celebrate the moment. I've learned that's all I really have. What a powerful force we are. I am convinced that gravity is really not the force that holds us on this earth; it is the gossamer (not sure of the spelling) threads that connect us. To me you are living proof of my theory...the world according to Spejcher.

Glad to hear you are on the mend, Jack. Love and hugs to both of you!

Nancy S.

Happy Valentine's Day!!

Dreamcatchers and Dolphins

 Dear Marsha and Jack,

Thanks once again for updating your friends at Communitas of the details of your journey. While on the plane to Wichita, KS, this week I wrote the following poem – surely being influenced by the events of your past few months.

In Search of Community

Where is community? I asked
Is it future? Is it past?
Where is community? Came the reply -
It is ground. It is sky.

What is community? I then wondered.
Is it up? Is it under?
What is community? I heard it cry.
It is presence. It can never die.

How is community? I still proposed.
Is it poetry? Is it prose?
How is community? Came back my quest.
It is here. A welcome guest.

Why is community? Again I sighed.
Why is community? It still replied.
The silence is broken by the sound of a bell.
Community echoes at the bottom of your well.

Ernie P.

Marsh and Jack!!

I am dancing with joy! Positive thoughts, and tremendous support from the cyberspace circle ...together we overcome!! Don't forget in all of this, that the support you received is because of the tremendous support, teaching and love you both give!!

Love to you both

Bev K.

Dreamcatchers and Dolphins

Marsh,

    You are playing on such a vast stage at the minute, I'm almost too humble to walk on for a bit part...But I have got something to send you from across the sea that struck a match in me. It's a poem by Siegfried Sassoon called "Everyone Sang".

> Everyone suddenly burst out singing.
> And I was filled with such delight
> As prisoned birds must find in freedom
> Winging wildly across the white
> Orchards and dark-green fields; on; on; and out of
> sight
>
> Everyone's voice was suddenly lifted,
> And beauty came like setting sun.
> My heart was shaken with tears; and horror
> Drifted away......O but everyone
> Was a bird; and the song was wordless; the singing
> Will never be done"

    This reminds me of many times, and one of them is the day last May when you both led the conference in song at the end. It also says the song won't stop now and anyway it's too late to stop now. (and as you say there's so much work to be done)

    I've resisted having heroes for a long time but you guys are seriously threatening this resolve ....
    kind thoughts from a fan of yours.

Derek W.

Marsha Forest & Jack Pearpoint

 Marsha & Jack,

Marsha, you might recall (on the way to the Barrier reef) our discussions of cancer & illnesses and how we deal with them. Lynne, my wife and travelling companion (reaching into its 3rd decade) had a cerebral aneurysm. This meant: opening her skull; clipping 2 minute blood vessels; closing it all up; and then trying to help her recover both physically & mentally. Physical was in the hands of the "body-technicians" and the Gods. Mentally was left to us. We made it (but not without a lot of work), just in time to discover ovarian cancer and what all that entails. Now that Lynne's been "topped & tailed", as she calls it, we live with the day-to-day knowledge that there is yet another aneurysm "up there" that they can't surgically get to (at least not without killing her trying). Minus the trauma; nothing has changed; yet all has changed. We didn't stop travelling – we do it more. We didn't stop our work – we probably do even more, but we now do it all with a much more healthy appreciation of our vulnerability ... and in that we have been given the insight of the vulnerability and pain in others.

From the husband-side of the equation, I learned of the loneliness. Of course we didn't have the Internet then; and our families were on the opposite side of the planet. But even with friends around, all of the healing & other "energies" are rightly focussed on the one who is ill. I was fortunate to learn to be comfortable with my aloneness. However, I too needed some of the healing. Marsha, it may be that you will have to help others to include Jack in the healing energies. We also learned another frightening (albeit now empowering) thing from our too frequent trips to the "body-mechanics" and doctors. Even

241

tho' they dress the same, there are some people in those body-healing places who are damn good doctors and others who are possibly even better body-mechanics, but will never be "real doctors" (or at least real "healers") because they have an "attitude handicap". That is, society has put a barrier in their way ... it's not an impairment (well I don't have any genetic data anyway!) but never-the-less they have been handicapped by society's having elevated their skill into a "god-like" status and they have naively or consciously decided to play this role. You will probably recognise this distinction from your experiences thus far???? The frightening part is that we trust everything they tell us as "gospel" ... the empowering thing is that we have learned that we must become "experts" on the condition and become the quality safeguards to ensure our life is given it's **best** chance of survival. Maybe this story will serve as an example:

When Lynne had brain surgery I read all I could; not just about aneurysms, but about the various treatment methods. I asked the doctors all the way, what they were going to be doing ...exactly. (Of course this was not accomplished without a lot of "assertiveness" but eventually they got "used to me" and even began telling me about the procedure before I asked.) I dealt with "trust me" by replying, "In God I trust .. all others please explain". If they said they were too busy, I said, "Add the 2 minutes to my bill." (They never did). Only recently this information saved Lynne's life. She went for a check up and neurosurgeon ordered a magnetic scan of her brain. I said, "Don't you have to do an angiogram?" (He was most put out at my question!) He huffed & puffed and told me about the dangers of this test compared to that and I said, "Sure, I'd love you to do the less intrusive test .. only one problem, Lynne's aneurysm was clipped the year before plastic clips were invented. If you use the magnetic test on her, it will unclip the aneurysm because YOU used metal clips." In a much heated display, he opened his records and discovered I was right. No apology. Body mechanic.

Be vigilant, enjoy life.

Kindest regards.

Darrell W.

Dreamcatchers and Dolphins

 Marsh and Jack,

Can you believe I was actually foolish enough to not write because I thought you might be getting too much mail and would be tired of it? I guess we all have our down days, but I finally woke up. So here I am telling you that I'm still with you, and adding my cheer to what now must be a roar — the cheer heard round the world I'm sure.

I'm so glad to hear the results of the breast cancer and I have loudly told the ovarian cancer to get out of your body. I started as a Phys. Ed. teacher so I can really yell when I want to!

Marsha and Jack, I'm sure your story, and the process of your coping with your lives, has been a powerful message for many of us. I, of course cannot help but relate your experiences to my own recent health problems. Like you, I did a lot of writing and shared it with those closest to me. What a powerful tool.

You wanted stuff to read Marsha. Have you read Rupert Ross' *Dancing With A Ghost*? You likely have - but if not, do. I also just read the newest *Educational Leadership*. Perhaps you haven't had a chance to see it yet, but there's a really interesting article called the Neurobiology of Self-Esteem and Aggression. I'll let you read it, but basically it provides an argument for Inclusion from a physiological/neurobiological point of view. Everything I've ever seen on Inclusion comes from the "socially correct" angle, so to me it was new.

See you soon. Still with you ... all the way.
Barb H.

February 16, 1997

Good Morning Whanau..

Dearest *Whanau*,

Writing in the morning will give this letter a different tone, as I am different at various parts of the day. Somehow the word 'lyrical' comes to mind for me right now. Snow covers the tops of the trees outside. It is a grey wintry day and lyrical, quiet, and thoughtful for me. Jack, who is finally over his horrible flu, has gone to Computerfest with three of Cathy's crew (Daddy Dave, Jonathan and Joel). This could be a dangerous trip financially, as who knows what Jack will find.

My trusty white, worn and loved polar bear, named "polar bear", sits in the crook of my arm as I ponder the past month, think of the present and look to the future. As relieved as I feel, I am also still really scared; and so I write to say I still need all of you – and will for a long time (I hope). Once again Shafik hit me over the head with his wise words, when I spoke to him last night. He reminded me that, although one battle is in control, I am living with cancer, a cell disease, and that vigilance is going to be the word to guide me for years to come. He knows.

I wish I did not have this other shadow on the CT scan to worry about, but most likely there will always be that worry lurking around. That is my life now and as Cathy so aptly puts it, "This is your life. Deal with it." Basically that's it in a nutshell. There is no other choice, there is no other way. This is now my life and to survive it, and even thrive in it, I have

245

chosen to reach out to all of you and use these experiences to teach myself, and hopefully others, how to live with what life deals us. "TEACH WHAT YOU WANT TO LEARN," say the sages.

We have an overhead (projection) that says, "Change is inevitable, growth is optional." I thought of a variation that says, "Death is inevitable, life is optional." I choose life for as long as it is granted to me, and believe me I value everyday in every way. I had a vanilla latte yesterday, West Coast style (this means weaker than Italian style). It was a peak experience! Little things suddenly mean even so much more.

There is a paradox in so much I see and think about these days. For example: I am awed by the power of the circle to heal, but aware that we must be very careful not to then blame ourselves, or the circle, if someone gets sick or dies. The circle is there to give strength, energy and hope. We cannot blame those who, for whatever reasons, don't get well or don't reach out for help. I am angered by simplistic comments that people **choose** the sicknesses they get or that they have **control** over their own life and death. That is true to some extent. One can choose how to react to certain events, but one certainly doesn't choose all the events. Most of us mere mortals want to live, to love, be loved and to be healthy.

The word that sums up how I feel is *human*. When people say how strong or brave we are, it doesn't ring true for me. All I feel is human, fragile, vulnerable. Sometimes strong, sometimes fragile, sometimes positive, sometimes scared. I feel it all – that's what human means to me. I can't live up to the popular expectation to "feel positive" in the face of some simply terrifying stuff. I do know that love and true comradeship are high on my list of why people survive tests of endurance. Alone we're sunk. Together we at least have a fighting chance! It's also more fun – together.

Also, for those of you who know me, be clear that I am not getting religious. I am definitely deepening spiritually, but that is very different. In fact this morning is a lovely example of this. I am surrounded by falling snow, a beautiful basket of tulips, my eagle feather, Jack's incredible photos and a library of books. These symbols are for me part of the spirit I feel. Those of you who are religious I truly value. I value deeply my truly Christian, Jewish or Moslem friends, as well my atheist or agnostic friends. I like to remind people that I am Jewish in my very own way (that's allowable for Jews – no two Jewish people hold the same views on anything) and for me it is people and nature, particularly the mountains and the ocean, that give me a feeling I don't get anywhere else.

The most helpful people, these past 6 weeks, have been the listeners and the cheerleaders – and Jack of course has elements of both (lucky me). The listeners really hear. They listen to the fear, hear the terror, feel the loneliness of the little girl, and at the heart of it all – the fear of death and dying. They listen. They wait for the tears to come out. They offer an ear. They do not attempt to solve anything. They are there. They are present. They give their advice and suggestions from their souls, with never a "should" attached to it, nor with a threat that if I don't do it, something bad will happen.

The cheerleaders and coaches offer themselves. Let's walk,

or shop, or work. Cathy is amazing in this area. She comes in and we work. Shannon has me on a vitamin program. We see these next years as a metaphor of me as a marathon runner. Marathons take training and as Jack (my chief trainer) says, I am allowed some down days and time off once in awhile (but not often.) Even marathoners have injuries – take healing breaks – then resume their training...

Jack of course is my heartbeat and soul partner. Unthinkable to be without one another. That is the vulnerability of love. It is what makes the tears really flow. It is what keeps me going on those really tough days.

Then there is work. Work and the bigger picture – so I don't get caught in my own petty concerns. Work to change the world to one where everyone can have a decent and just quality of life. My political warrior friends are my mentors on that front. A resistance movement against the mean spiritedness out there which blames people for everything wrong and doesn't want to look deep into the heart of a system, with greed at its base, as the real culprit of so many societal ills. That bigger picture also keeps me going as I feel I am part of a movement for change which needs me and all our voices.

So I am humble in asking you to please stick with me. Keep up those chants, prayers, wishes, dreams – whatever – for the **Ovarian Cancer** is the scary one to keep under control. It is the shadow of fear that I still have to learn to live with.

Josie Hill told me, that one of her elders told her to tell me, "...to talk to my body and **demand** the cancer get lost. So you can all help by sweeping, yelling and doing whatever it takes to

impolitely tell the cancer to get lost. Those of you who are too polite may refrain from this exercise. I will ask Gerv from Nottingham in his best rugby voice to lead the charge on this front. I know he will agree.

The plan now is to see the breast doctor on Wednesday (for a check up). Then get on a plane (Thurs.) for a long and wonderful journey to Anchorage, Alaska. Then Yellowknife and back home March 10. Then the radiation plan goes into effect (dates to be determined). I am OK on that front. It will be as it will be. The fear is only that something else will show up, but that is a fear I am learning to live and deal with.

I am thrilled that so many people have written and that our letters have encouraged our friends to call their own circles together. I reflected this morning that many years ago when I got divorced, (a very traumatic event for anyone), I phoned my parents after I had arrived at this difficult decision. After! Imagine that – I had told no one. I can't even imagine it. I was ashamed. I couldn't face my failure. Those scars remain. I blame no one, but I see how far I have come in reaching out for help and not thinking I have to go it alone. No one does!

Dave Hingsburger, a brilliant writer and thinker especially dealing with people suffering from abuse and institutionalization, has been writing incredible words of wisdom; and encouraging me to put this all in a book. He says, "Your journey will show those who love and care for someone facing tough medical issues how they can respond. People want to show love but really need examples of how to do so."

Dream Catchers and Dolphins

So true. If my story can assist others in their own circles of life I will be thrilled. I think the tragedy is the person who is alone. And yet the world is full of one very plentiful resource: *'tis people, 'tis people, 'tis people.*

At the moment, I wish I could get back some of the joyful energy I know is in me. I am surrounded by so much beauty in this home we have created. On my PATH now I look forward to a walk today, a visit with friends, and Jack each night next to me, plus all your continued support. I hope this conveys the thanks and love I feel for all of you. My wishes are with you too. I take a few reflective moments each day to send all my energies of health and joy to all of you and your families. Our community is not a one way street. It is a busy thoroughfare where the energy of the traffic flows in many directions.

We have survived another difficult phase. My line is: "We will get through this." It is not: "I will get through this." Truly WE are the key.

Thanks and love. I hope this all makes sense. I am thinking through many issues and I welcome your thoughts as well.

And now for some more on the Yiddish lessons front: For those of you too shy to ask the meaning of "punim and pupik" (from the Common Jewish Expressions book), a punim means 'face' and a pupik means 'bellybutton'. A colloquial English translation would now be, "You don't know your punim from your pupik....or your backside from a hole in the ground."

The following is a wonderful story on community building,

and why we all need to get back to our roots of asking one another to listen to our stories. This ancient community building story comes from Harold Eiser who told Arthur Naiman this tale for his Jewish Expressions book. "There was a common custom in the shtetl (small rural settlement Eastern European Jews lived in – like the town in Fiddler on the Roof) when a woman had all she could tolerate of her family problems, she would walk out into the middle of the street and bang on her teakettle *(HOK A CHAINIK)*. Hearing this, the neighbouring housewives would come out and listen while she told them her troubles. When she got it all off her chest, everybody would go home again." Isn't that wonderful. And we thought some Western psychologist had invented group therapy! So thank you all for letting me *Hok a Chainik* and I encourage you to bang your teakettle to those you choose – it is a lifesaving exercise. Today we can do it with modern technology – fax and e-mail.

Time for a bubble bath – another wonder of the modern world.

Arohanui,
Marsha – and Jack who is finally **not** coughing.

Dreamcatchers and Dolphins

Marsha & Jack:

Thanks for all the sharing you do. I don't have any particularly wise or appropriate words, but do want you to know that I am a listener and occasionally a cheerleader.

I do want to say something about about bravery and vulnerability, something that I expect that you already know or at least that you are beginning to feel. These are not mutually exclusive terms. True bravery only begins when we understand our vulnerability. The soldier who goes into battle believing he is invulnerable is not brave, merely psychotic.

There is no bravery above allowing yourself to feel your human instincts, and telling others what you feel. Your instincts have served you well for a very long time and they will not fail you now.

Best regards

Dick Sobsey

Good morning Thunder,

I just smiled as I read your last thoughts to your villagers. I could see through your eyes where you were sitting/laying and watching the snow, and I love gray, wintry days. These kind of days allow me to slow down ... and think ... and think good thoughts. I'm jealous.

But what made me smile even more was seeing you being so willing now to share. I am talking about your sharing of your "fear", Thunder. I'm not talking about your sharing the "fact" of your cancer. People can't fix that thing they don't understand. I think you are getting near to the point where you are going to be able to "fix" your fear.

This doesn't mean that you won't have fear, it simply means that you'll concentrate less upon it; and realize that while you have life, you will live this life instead of living the fear. It means that you won't allow the weight of your possible (and always present) death determine how you'll live your gift of life. It means that you'll move on and began to speak more of "life", than of death ... I am also clear that you are concerned with being away from Lightening, and how'd he'd be with that. What beautiful love Thunder, what a beautiful expression of love. What's the answer? You don't need an answer ... you only need to know that there is one – and that together all of us who love Thunder and Lightening will figure it out.

Remember Thunder, death is merely a chapter in that great book of life, I refuse to see it any other way ... and by the way, when you get the chance, give my love to Lightening (I like that dude).

one who's been caught,
Shafik

Dreamcatchers and Dolphins

Marsh,

I received your "Good morning Whanau" message tonight. A corner has been turned. It is not dramatic, but it is profound. I have listened to you for years. I have heard the raging warrior that spoke over top of the frightened and lonely child. Tonight I heard the blossoming elder. A gentleness, that has been growing through the winter of your years with cancer, is breaking through like the crocus. I am happy to hear you tonight. Not that you have had to live through the attack that cancer has waged on your body, but in spite of the interruptions it has brought to your dance, you and Jack live, and choose to live again and again.

It is true that in a world that seems bent on dying and death, we need to see visible reminders that life is a choice, no matter what other message falls upon our path. Your nakedness in sharing your journey, and your humanness, is a sacrament. "Sacrament" is a word from my own Catholic roots. I recall its meaning to be a visible sign of God's presence among us. I think of the word, I think of you, and I remember Father Pat Mackan. I know he is smiling with pride as he heard your thoughts, and read your letter.

Your message reminds me of the quote:
"Courage is fear held on a moment longer."

There is no Hollywood romantic heroism here, simply an accessible, vulnerable choice. While your life situation, resources, education, etc., may differ from many people, your example of choosing life and reaching out to those who are around you, is one that is available to most, however small the beginnings might be. It is a story that needs to be heard.

My life is richer for having listened, read, and seen your journey up close and personal.

Thanks.

Dave Hasbury

Dreamcatchers and Dolphins

Marsha,

I'm so glad that you and Jack have come through this far in what must have been the most threatening time of your life. I have thought of you often and in doing so have revisited some places where I am always uneasy about going. Your e-mail keeps saying that we shouldn't allow ourselves to be alone. That's true of course. Sharing pain, fear and anxiety with others, who pull together with you in a crisis, is the basis of true community. Isn't it crazy though, that the spirit of real community seems to need some sort of a crisis before we see it materialize and take shape?

There's no denying that circles in our lives so often mark the difference between survival and death, I understood that very plainly when Sheila died. Then, the power of people coming together raised me to a plain of safety – when I needed it most. Now I am a few years down the road from that very personal life trauma and I am beginning to understand that I cannot expect circles alone will, in themselves, be the complete answer to all our ills. There is no getting away from the fact that there are some things that we simply have to deal with ourselves alone and that even the best circle of friends can only take us so far in helping us to tackle the root of the fear that embeds itself inside of us. First we have to survive; and friends who unite themselves around us make that possible. Just by being there, they show us how we can find the power to get by and the energy to search for answers. But at the end of the day there is really only one person who can deal with the cold monsters within. I am still struggling to find the strength and courage to slay my own particular dragons. With the help of friends, some days I am stronger than others. And as time passes, I really do become more empowered to understand myself better and find that my feelings of sadness and fears are not nearly so intimidating as they used to be. In fact, now I sometimes even find them amusing. Yes it is wonderful when friends form a circle of strength around you, but recognize too that only you can clearly see and feel those things that haunt you and only you can overcome them. When you do you will reach a place of peace that shines with an incandescence, the like of which you have never known. Who knows, perhaps those who have not had the good fortune to make it through a major crisis can never truly know just how wonderful life really is.

Thank you Marsha for giving me the power of your concern and friendship when I needed it most. I will always love you and Jack for that. I live because of it. Sadness, pain and fear are unwelcome bedfellows and I know that you will not choose to tolerate them. You are such a strong woman, Marsha, and I am so proud of you.

Big big love,

Kenn J.

Dreamcatchers and Dolphins

 Good Morning Jack and Marsha!

For several days my E-Mail was not working so you can imagine my surprise when all of your mail rolled off on Friday. I spent a long time reading and pondering your words and was overwhelmed with the blessings I received. Thank you for honouring me with your thoughts and allowing me to enter your circle of love. As well as keeping you in my prayers, I also remember all those who are sending their love through faxes, parcels and E-mails.

Because you shared with me, you have already helped another person who has been battling cancer for the last several months. A number of us have been trying to provide support, but she is a very private person and wasn't letting anyone in. I told her about your letters and your circle which was sending energy from around the world and suggested she might like to read what you wrote. Thank you for giving permission to share! I believe there is hope now!

Once again, thank you for honouring and blessing me as you have done. I will be with you on this journey. May God bless you, always.

Pat also sends her love!

Madonna F.

Marsha Forest & Jack Pearpoint

Kia ora whanau,

Wow, I can only imagine all that snowstorm and shiver! It's another beautiful day here; and it is made better by your strength – knowing that you are well into the next work and living to the fullest again. That's what draws people to you Marsha – it's all that energy. But as you told me it could be negative because others expect you to be that way all the time. That is why when you share your fears you share an inner strength that only those who really know you can appreciate.

Shafik, as a fellow 'harbourer of mutant cells' and another true warrior, knows the physical, the mental and the spiritual highs and lows that you are going through. It is so wonderful that you have each other to battle on that level. You both must work to make a difference to others who are less fortunate. And might I add that Judith is another of that warrior band.

That's all the goes this round – have a great trip to Alaska

Miss and love you

Sister Te

259

Dreamcatchers and Dolphins

February 18, 1997

Common Ground...Off to Alaska

Dear Friends,

I was sitting with a friend today and crying over my fear and worry when I said, "I just don't know how I'm supposed to deal with all this. How am I supposed to do this? How am I **supposed to** be?" I suddenly smiled. My friend burst out into a gentle laugh. I started to laugh. It was like some lovely cosmic joke and I finally had a glimpse into the absurdity of the whole mess we call life. I had a flash of real insight. Not the cheap short range type, but the big bang type of insight.

"I suddenly realized there really is no **supposed to** here. I can only do what I can do. I can only be who I am. I can only do this in my way, whatever that way happens to be. There is no route that someone else will carve out for me. I (who am one of the developers of a tool called PATH) have to take my own rhetoric more seriously; and create my own PATH though life, which includes the good and bad times." I was now laughing quite vigorously which felt really good. I then started to cry again, which also felt good. I was indeed doing the 'Te Ripowai dance of life' - laughing and crying and letting the mucus flow. And as I did so, I got my appetite back and also some of that fighting spirit which has for fifty years allowed me to live my life without the "supposed to's" – but at a cost.

It is so simple
It is so hard to do.

So I realize – it is I (with a little help from my friends) who must find the path in this era of my life. There is opportunity in crisis they say. Actually I say that a lot. The obvious opportunity for me now is to get rid of the "shoulds", "coulds", "woulds", and "oughts" and most of all the "supposed to's."

"How am I supposed to feel, act and be.
I guess it is now totally up to me."

I know one thing for sure. I will not succumb to this damn cell disease or crawl into bed and stay there! Although there are times I will crawl into bed – to rest and get strength for the battles ahead. That is different.

Something I am saying is certainly hitting a chord for some people out there in the land of the readers. And I really like the people who that chord is resounding with. There is an incredible synergy and energy happening from that chord. Mark Vaughan doing his overtone chanting in the Taj Mahal is symbolic of the beauty of the chant. Poetry and amazing writing is coming my way. Deep thoughtful stories, full of pain and joy. Something is going on out there. And certainly something is really going on inside me. The healing from wounds – very old and very new.

Our small, and yet mighty, community of diversity around the world is really not such a small force after all. Look out! There is Rosemary Crossley tearing down institutional walls in Australia. The Nottingham band is changing life for so many kids and families in England. All the resistance fighters in the USA and Canada are out there working day and night. We are not such a small circle. And as Gunnar Dybwad reminds us, when we unite with the Human Rights Movement, we are

Dream Catchers and Dolphins

indeed a large force.

OK – back to my conversation with my friend. I pondered, "What is a healthy person?" My friend felt it was people who could undergo trauma and difficulty, process it and then get on with their lives. Holding onto pain and trauma of any kind does not produce healing. The reverse is to let the trauma go (after really examining it), setting a PATH with meaning, and going on that PATH for as long as one can.

Since I was still into exploring the tyranny of the "supposed to's," I decided to make my own unique "supposed to" list. (This may be more endemic to females but I am open to suggestion on this issue.)

OK – the "supposed to" voices in my head tell me that I am "Supposed to":
* feel good all the time
* pretend to feel good when I don't
* solve all my problems by myself, or with my husband, and not with a psychologist or, God forbid, a psychiatrist - that would mean I was really sick ... and they only turn you against your family anyway...
* not get sick - sick happens to others not to the chosen few (i.e., me)
* keep any problems private and secret
* be calm at all times or appear to look calm
* never be tired or appear to look tired
* never yawn
* always be smart and know a lot
* be polite and nice

* always be helpful
* be a great cook
* always be creative
* always be "on"
* always be "on top" of things
* feel good and make others feel good
* always say "yes"

I am going to toss this "supposed to" list in the fire and attempt to be aware of not living up to my list. Polarities hurt us all. They hurt me.

> strong vs. weak.
> public vs. private.
> up vs. down.
> courageous vs. cowardly.

I am all of the above. It is natural to be frightened, and scared. It is also natural to be courageous and strong. Which side wins is partly a matter of being surrounded by people who can pull out the **good** stuff while accepting the **whole** picture. Even the most courageous freedom fighters are scared some of the time. They do not, however, let the fear dominate. But they also don't pretend it isn't there.

Courageous and caring people are all out there – waiting to be asked to be compassionate, caring, and warm. Most of us never ask and are never asked. That is why inclusive education and inclusive communities are so powerful. It is about real people, with real needs, reaching out to each other to help one another out of the hole we call life. It is not talking about compassion and caring. It is **doing** it and figuring out how to do it as we go along.

Dream Catchers and Dolphins

We all do know certain things. We know children die, or do not thrive, when they are not loved and held. When a child has no intimacy, she literally starves for affection. We know the early effects of abuse and neglect are often never overcome. Why is this different for most adults? I say it is not.

Secrets and Lies, as the movie of that title so brilliantly portrays, kill the spirits of all involved in the deception. And yet being honest, about who we truly are, is a lifelong struggle. Other films that portray this are: *Shine* (Australia) and the most powerful film from New Zealand, *Once Were Warriors*. All these films passionately portray the universal truths of what abuse, neglect, and oppression of any kind does to the human spirit. They also show the power of real ordinary community (people) to change the system and to change one another's lives. The power of love is enormous – and bigger than we dream.

So this human spirit (that's me) has reached out and will continue to reach out through her writing to keep her own life going, and in this way perhaps help others out of the particular 'holes' in which they find themselves.

Once again, my brother Shafik hit the mark in his most recent e-mail message. He writes, "What made me smile in reading your words was seeing you so willing to share. I am talking about your willingness to share your "fear," Thunder, I am not talking about the cancer. I think you are getting near to the point where you can "fix" your fear. That doesn't mean that you won't have fear, it simply means that you'll concentrate less on it and realize that while you have life, you will live this life instead of living the fear. It means you won't let the weight of your possible and always present death determine how you'll live your gift of life. It means you will move on and begin to speak more of "life" than of death..."

And another friend, Dave Hasbury, writes so beautifully and says that my letter reminded him of the quote, that "Courage is fear held on a moment longer." David also touched me deeply when he said, "Your nakedness in sharing your journey, and your humanness, is a sacrament. *Sacrament* is a word from my own Catholic roots. I recall its meaning to be a visible sign of God's presence among us. I think of the word, I think of you, and I remember Father Pat Mackan, our friend and mentor. I know he is smiling with pride as he heard your thoughts, and read your letter."

So as I sit here. Still vulnerable, and still scared that the doctor will say that I can't go to Alaska. Still scared that something else will happen. Still scared about that shadow on the CT scan. Still scared about the blood tests results. I know deep down I will be on that plane Thursday and many other planes – carrying an even more passionate and powerful message to those we work with. I know this deep in my guts. I know it, as I know those 9 turtles I swam with in Cozumel and who escorted me through my surgery less than 2 weeks ago.

I want to end this night letter with the four lines sent to me by Charlie Galloway, a lovely friend in California. He was listening to the music on the radio when, as he says, these lyrics penetrated the distractions. Charlie writes, "The tune was Latinesque, kinda Brazilian-bouncy and the chorus went like this:

Dream Catchers and Dolphins

> In a circle of friends
> In a circle of sound
> All our voices will blend
> When we find common ground.

And I took these words and amended them slightly to say:

> In our circle of friends
> In our circle of sound
> All our voices are blending
> We are finding common ground.

Good night.

With love again,

Marsha and from Jack as well.

Alaska bound!!! Yes!

Dear Marsha,

From your recent note I am getting vibes that you are healthy, your spirit is healing!

God, your words had such a sound of resonance to me. Particularly the "should be" list. I have had my own list that I have had to wage battle with. Imagine it, this totally experienced professional in disability and inclusion gets a child with a disability for her very own! Oh, the "should be's" just flowed! Yes, I was supposed to know it all! My God, if anyone can do this it is you, Sharon! God, picked you special cause he knew you could help your son. Your problems will be taken care of because you know what to do above anyone else. Blah, blah blah. I heard it all and I said it all in my head. I was never supposed to cry out; be afraid or angry or any thing, not SHARON!!!! It is bullshit, Marsha.

Luke, my precious boy, has opened up my spirit to heal too (I did not realize how much I needed it). There are days I break into tears; days I cry out with anger; days my fears become monsters; days of jubilance; days of sunlight. It is the stuff of life, Marsha. This is what I have learned.

I know you are a spiritual person. I believe in a God. And in delivering me to this thing called life, he never promised there would be no fear – pain – suffering. But I have at times acted as if it were so. That somehow my life was to be neat and tidy always. I don't think God specially "chose" me to have Luke, any more than he chose you to have cancer. It happens. The control monster you and Jack have written and spoken about so frequently with inclusion??? It is the same control monster that deluded me into thinking that life could always be so neat and tidy. My real transformation came when I stopped dwelling within the question, "why me" and began to consider, "why not me?" Somehow everything changes with that question. The next logical question is, "so now that this has happened, what shall I do, how will I live my life, and on and on?"

I have often tried to describe to people my experience at living life with Luke. Everything is amplified. Joy is so much more joyous. Sad is ever so much sadder. It is a certain rawness that pervades. I remember when he was three weeks old and the doctor had just called to say that my Luke was missing part of his brain. I sat there in the rocking chair and felt something so very different than I had ever experienced before. Here I was so very incredibly happy to have my child in my arms and such profound sadness at the same time for knowing his life would be a struggle. It is a vulnerability to feel things at such intensity. It is like having a layer of skin removed, raw nerves exposed. I don't know if this is what you are feeling but reading your words made me think of that day so vividly.

In a book called, *From the Heart: Stories by Mothers of Children with Special Needs,* there is a poem. It only says it is from Kathy.

> "In the essential sadness of all of this is the Glory.
> Everything that is wonderful about that child,
> all of the love and devotion I feel for my child
> is not separate from the sadness,
> it isn't just the badness
> it is painful joy,
> or joyful pain,

the two are together."
    Painful joy, joyful pain - the two are together. I think it is
called life.

    All of my love, devotion, prayers, and gratitude

Sharon G.

Dreamcatchers and Dolphins

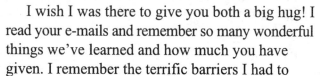

My dearest Marsha & Jack,

I wish I was there to give you both a big hug! I read your e-mails and remember so many wonderful things we've learned and how much you have given. I remember the terrific barriers I had to overcome, that summer in Montreal, to admit that I, too, sometimes must seek the kindness and comfort of others. I want you to know my life was forever changed. That summer and the times we've seen each other since then have left me with greater knowledge, but most of all **hope** for all the good things life has to offer.

Daily I see pain and suffering in my work with kids and their families. I also see great courage and hope. The courage is like some magnificent act of nature that moves towards the miracles and the dreams. Somewhere, deep inside me, is a reminder of the first workshop I ever attended that you gave. It seems so far away from who I am now. I do remember thinking, Marsha Forest can't really believe in inclusion, but I went anyway. After only one workshop, I was so excited. I couldn't wait to meet you and talk to and learn from you. I wanted to reach out to people I had never known before and touch them. I wanted to be their friend and I wanted them to be as much a part of this world as I am. Because of this workshop, I gained a whole new group of friends. They were no longer the "people with disabilities". They were my friends and what a world it opened up for me! Because of this, my life has been richer.

I've come a long way since those first days. It's hard to believe it's been 7 years! I remember the first time I did a training for a high school peer support group and introduced them to friendships they never would have experienced otherwise. I remember that afterwards, my daughter who attended that training, got sent to the office. You see, she stopped to help another student pick up some flowers she had dropped. My daughter wanted to know why she hadn't seen this student around school before this. The student politely told her, it was because she was in 'special ed' classes. "You see I have a lot of behaviour problems and don't learn very well." I am proud to say my daughter marched into the counsellor's office and demanded that her new friend be put into a regular classroom. The counsellor told Jacqui the student belonged in 'special ed' because of her behaviour problems. She responded, "My mom would say there is no excuse for separating kids."

Jacqui was so persistent in her request that the counsellor sent her to the office and the principal called me. How proud I was of her that day! I reiterated what Jacqui had said and told the principal about inclusion. Reluctantly, he gave me the opportunity to share information on inclusion with the 'special ed' teachers. Since that time, changes have been made. Still not total inclusion, but significant changes. Also, we received permission to film a video at the school. The video was not as important as what happened. Lots of friendships developed between the kids with disabilities and the kids who came to be in the film. It was joyful to watch! I know you hear stories like this all the time. You need to hear them. You need to know how much we love you and what an impact you have on the world.

Yes, I understand your vulnerability and your fears; and I pray with you, and for you, and send destruction vibes to the cancer. But, most of all, I know the type of lady you are. I know your courage, your strength, your compassion and your faith. All over the world there is our circle of friends and we do sound our voices to gather the tribes. Visualize the circle surrounding you with love, courage and strength. Visualize the light warming you, destroying the cells. Visualize the tribes beating their drums in unison with the beat of your heart. Visualize all those whose lives you have touched – moving toward you offering their miracles. Let it be our gift to you. We are your circle. Trust us. Walk without fear in our midst. You taught us well and we love you.

My prayers are with you daily.

Love,

Sandy W.

Marsha Forest & Jack Pearpoint

Marsha,

I hope you are having a wild and wonderful time in Alaska... or wherever you might be in your travels and work right now.

I want to share a few thoughts I've had as a result of belonging to the community of souls that have been expressing themselves so beautifully.

Marsha, you got to a level of life, through your fear of death, that few travel or know about. And you went one step further with your fear – you shared it with all of us. And because of your decision to be so real and so honest, many of us now know something greater that lives within you, and within all of us, that we would never have known without you sharing your truth. Thank you for that Marsha.

You have reframed my view of "surviving cancer" and pointed out a great irony for me. What I have witnessed in you is not at all about "surviving", it is about "living". Living with a new and greater freedom to express all of life. The irony is that there are those of us who have not dealt with our "cancer" (a thing which eats at our lives). We either don't see it or we don't stop and say "I want to live". We are really the ones surviving instead of living.

I want to add my personal encouragement to both of you. You need to be there for each other – raw, real and unfolded. The same way you have been for the community of spirits and souls that you have brought together.

Dream Catchers and Dolphins

Continue the journey, do the work, demand health, and be outrageous.

With love and passion for the Thunder and Lightning of life.

Your friend

Darleen S.

Marsha Forest & Jack Pearpoint

March 3, 1997

On the Road Again...

Dear E-mail Buddies,

We are currently en route from Anchorage to Vancouver via Seattle and then on to Yellowknife. I love airports. I love flying. I love life. Flying affords me the time to sit and look out windows on clouds. I always find the sky awesome and revealing. I also marvel at man/woman's incredible ability and talent to put these jumbo flying machines in the air. It is truly a testament to what is possible. Many thought flying a mere folly; and not that long ago at that. So I contemplate the clouds and I think that the real tragedy in life is not death, but in not living life fully and passionately when and while one can. We are living each day with meaning and passion.

Our work in Anchorage went really splendidly. It seems the "tools for change" and the "tools for teams", we are teaching and sharing, are hitting just the right chords. People in general want to change, to care, to do good. But many are stuck in old ways. The tools, particularly the graphics, the music, us as a team, MAPS, PATH, CIRCLES, etc. give people permission to do what they know has to be done. We hit the heart. We simply remind people what is really important. Then we offer tools that remind people to talk and to listen to one another. Not debate. Not discuss. Not argue. Instead, real dialogue, from the heart to the ear and back again and again. Real talk. Silence. Talk without words. Talk with real words. Communication... reciprocal and real.

275

Dream Catchers and Dolphins

As people have pointed out to us in these e-mail dialogues, many people want to help one another, but don't know how. Some of us with years of people skills, courses, and knowledge forget that there's more than common sense to real good communication. There are skills – and these skills can and must be taught. It is not enough to have the right values, the right intentions. It is important to have the knowledge and tools to make change possible. We are also seeing that we cannot revisit the mission and vision too often. We may take this for granted, But for others, reminding them of what they are really all about is the very first step. In some cases, it is enough to jolt the people back to the sanity of caring and out of the negativity and cynicism that surrounds so many people in education and human service work.

Using our own recent history in dealing with chronic cell disease, we can truly share the vision that "teams" and "circles" are tools for survival itself. The day before we arrived in An-chorage, a tragic murder occurred in the small Alaska town of Bethel. A teenager who had been suspended from High School came back and shot and killed a fellow student and the very loved school principal. The student's profile was classic – foster child, loner, labelled, isolated, abused. The community is calling not for the death of the student – but for healing. They are begging parents, teachers, and the students to talk to one another; not to keep secrets and lies. It seems the 'loner' told several other students of his plans. No one told anyone – hoping it would all go away. But we all know that bad stuff does not just go away. Arresting these students as accomplices to murder is one route. Figuring out why the students did not talk to one another is another route.

One of the keynote speakers at the conference was a wonderful Greek Orthodox priest, Father Michael Oleska, robed in black with a cap and a large wooden cross. His message was the same as ours: "We all need to belong." He asked the Shafik question, "Can we all just get along?" He was optimistic and felt the cultural diversity and pluralism of his home state of Alaska could be a model of many cultures learning not just to live together, but to celebrate life together.

The contrasts are enormous between what so many of us are saying, and what we see on a day to day basis. But the direction is clear. Diversity and pluralism are here to stay. Our mission is to bring the tools of change to people who want to change. We have no energy or desire to fight with people. We will of course fight politically, but personally in our work, if people don't like it, they can leave and come back another day. Few do.

Aside from work, we spent two days as tourists and got a real dose of the beauty of the Alaska landscape. We did a tour (by van and boat) of a piece of incredible scenery in Resurrection Bay. We saw glaciers, moose, eagles, mountain goats, etc. It was breathtaking, and for me, generates what a church or synagogue may offer others. On day 2, we did a glacier flight, over blue fields of ice, that truly took our breath away. Just three of us in a tiny plane flying quite low. The pilot, Jack and I loved every moment of seeing from the air what the motion of the earth creates in its core. One word. **Incredible**!!

This is what makes life worth living: our work; seeing the earth; and living each day. And this is life training – for when we return to Toronto we renew the marathon of making life possible. The radiation doctor meets with us on March 13th.

Dream Catchers and Dolphins

Then we go back to Dr. Michael Crump, the wonderful oncologist who found the breast cancer. He will plan the next schedule of events and hopefully not find anything else. We still don't know what the "shadow" on the CT scan is or the results of the blood tests. We are giving ourselves a rest. That appointment is March 18th. On March 17th – the breast check. (That at least is under control.) Keep those prayers, chants, songs, coming our way. As you can imagine, we are enjoying the break from the medical scene. On the other hand, without the medical excellence, there would be no other scene. The lesson is do what it takes, and don't ignore the tough stuff. Take care of first things first, then if you are lucky, you get to see the icy blue of the glacier.

We are now in Vancouver doing an overnight visit with Jack's family. His over eighty year old mother just made a great dinner for nine people. She is in great shape though partially deaf and legally blind. What do we see? The glass half full or half empty. The family dynamics are as usual, but we laugh at the rituals of the Pearpoints with love and affection, especially when we are here for a short and lovely visit.   We head to one of our favourite places (with some of our favourite people) next week, Yellowknife. There we will be shooting another *Inclusion Press* Video on "PATH IN ACTION" in a caring school system run by a rare Superintendent of Education (Ken Woodley), who we also consider a good friend. Stay tuned for more news on that front. In the meantime, thanks for being my Iditarod team. We learned much from watching and reading about the incredible team race of man/woman and dogs from Anchorage to Nome, Alaska. The Iditarod metaphor speaks to me now as I run this race of life with its ups and downs, highs and lows, periods of rest and work – mostly as I run through life with my team. It takes enormous work – this thing called life. It ain't always easy. But I know one thing for sure, without some people to truly hear your heart, you are sure to lose the race. No one in the Iditarod runs alone. It is teams of humans and animals together in a rare synchronicity that gets people across the finish line. Winning isn't the issue. Just getting through the race (over 1060 miles) is an enormous accomplishment. I don't believe anymore that some people are strong and some are weak. Some are gifted and others dull. I believe we all have capacity only in relationships, thus we are only as strong as our relationships grow and flourish. It is our job in life to tend our garden of relationships for without them we will die. With them, we at least have the best chance to enjoy life as long as any of us are able. There are no guarantees for any of us. The only guarantee is in the circle around us. Loneliness breeds the murder in Bethel, Alaska. Isolation and exclusion breed the secrecy and shame of sexual abuse and hurt. The answer is painfully simple to say, and excruciatingly difficult to implement. It is breaking the code of superman/ woman and saying "the emperor is really naked – superman/ woman doesn't exist." It is a dangerous myth. The answer lies in breaking the code of silence, in reaching out, in touching. I really understand why people drink and do drugs. I understand it at a deep gut level. I understand it because I have felt a terror and fear that is as deep as the icy blue glacier. Without people around me I would have gone under.

Yes, you can share your soul and still retain your private garden. Pieces of you that are yours can never be touched or really understood by anyone else. We are each unique. We are also the same. Our blood runs red. Our hearts beat as one heart. The Maori proverb runs through my veins today. It is why the

Dream Catchers and Dolphins

Tuhoe and I are brothers and sisters of the heart. I know that it is the words in the Maori proverb that will, in the long run, keep the human race alive.

"What is the greatest and most important thing in this world? I say to you, "Tis people, tis people, tis people."

Arohanui (much big love)
Marsha

PS – I had a bit of a real down this morning. Got scared real bad again and had a great hug with Jack and talked to our dear friend Duane (who is also a doctor). Did the tears and then I was OK. This reaching out stuff is really powerful. I think I am learning and teaching an important lesson.

PS Today is Sunday. It is sunny and 30 below zero in Yellowknife. We are having a blessed morning of sleeping in and reading until we begin our work in Yellowknife at 1:30 today when we get to film (and hopefully ride in) a dog sled. We decided that the dog teams are going to be the metaphor for our new video. One of the school principals here has a team of dogs so we get to try it out. Whoopee! Can't wait!

More on that later.

Marsha

March 10, 1997

Thinking About Stuff...

Dear Jack, John, Dave and Shafik,

So I'm in the bathtub and I'm thinking again about all this stuff about being positive and thinking positively. Basically I am an optimistic person. I believe the world has changed and will continue to change. I am not afraid of change although it is not easy, but I am having trouble with this being positive stuff.

For example. I am really happy to be home and cosy in wonderful artisitic and warm home. But I am not happy that I have to go to the doctors again, that I still don't know what is totally going on with the shadow on the CT scan, that I have to have radiation and have no idea of the schedule. So I am scared. I am sad, mad as well as glad to be home.

So when we tell people to be positive it seems so glib. Perhaps it is just me. That's OK too I've decided. If I am the only person on earth who feels this way than so be it. But I hunch that we often make people sicker and crazier when they think they are supposed to feel positive about things that are really difficult. This applies to having a sick child, having a child with difficulties in school, going through a divorce, being depressed etc.

I think for me what helps are a few universals:

a. I know I am loved and I love. This is the intimacy circle for me and it is one central person.

b. I know I am loved and I love a wider circle of friends. This is another layer of small but vital friends.

c. I know I am valued and I value a wide network of friends

and associates around the world who really care about me and Jack.

d. I have important and real work to do.

e. I have exciting plans for the future.

f. I have a comfortable and stable place to live.

g. I have enough money to not be worried about being on the street or hungry.

This is not a hierarchy of needs. This is my thoughts on a possible universal list of stuff any person needs to survive a crisis. It is not simply telling someone to be positive. It is asking myself and others if they have the ingredients in their life to make it possible to survive a crisis.

I have an attitude all right and it is not always positive. It is however a fighting spirit to survive as long as I am able by acting and doing what it takes to get better. What do you call that? I don't call it positive or negative. I call it being in touch with the earth I stand on.

I worry that someone may have a positive attitude and thus wait or be so nice as to not deal with issues that need immediate attention and thus they get hurt by being so nice and positive. How can anyone be positive about the cuts in health and education. I am mad about all that and hopeful that through political action and real democracy "we the people" will get back a government that believes in keeping all the people educated and well.

It is also a hard act to keep up being positive when you feel like hell, or scared, or sad. When people tell me how strong or positive I am I want to refer them to Jack who has seen the copious tears, who has himself felt the immensity of both our fears, who has seen not the weak or strong me but the real me.

That is the issue. If I didn't have a few people to be totally real with I would truly be sick in the spirit and soul. Total realness means being able to deal with the demons and then get on. It is amazing as I travel and tell my story first thing in the morning my energy is liberated to do the work we do even better than we've ever done it before.

It can't be scripted. I has to authentically come from the heart. It is also not asking others for help and that I think is the key. I am telling people that I have this issue I am dealing with (be it cancer,depression,divorce,whatever life crisis you wish to choose) and I do not need their help but welcome their support. That's that then we can go on.

The lesson here for all of us is not to go on and on and on with our problems (which bore people after awhile) but be solution minded and carry on with life as best we can. One woman put it very well, "I don't feel you dumped your problems on us and made us feel responsible for you or to solve your porblems. You just told us your reality and then we could all get on with the work at hand."

We recently did a workshop where two women sat crying in the circle. The leader of the group tried to carry on with the meeting at hand. It was impossible as everyone could see these two women in tears. Finally one of them told us what was going on. A young person they both knew had just been killed in an accident. Everyone could feel and share their pain. But by not stating the obvious they were affecting an entire room full of people. So they told their story and then they could choose to leave or stay and go on with the work.

The foolishness of pretending no one knows what is going on when everyone knows is the kind of crazy-making that wrecks families, organizations and even countries. How many suicides could be prevented if people felt they could talk to the key people in their lives.

I think this moving from private to public space is a tricky issue and one I am exploring as I once in awhile wonder at my sharing this stuff not only in e mail but in a book. It is easy for me to write about inclusion and change. It is harder to share my own story and yet I have been getting so much feed back about how important it is. What are your thoughts on this?

It also seems that as I share these issues I also put clearer boundaries around my garden as Dave Hinsberger wrote weeks ago. I will share the beauty and pain of my life but don't tread in my intimacy garden. Those who do will be politely told to step off. Most haven't. I think when you set boundaries people are clear and respect your wishes. I have been awed by the beauty, respect, and depth of the responses to my e mails. And pleased that most are not playing into the "sick" model and respecting the "I am healthy with a cell disease" definition I have chosen. Also most realize Thunder and Lightening come as a package and that support is for Jack as well as me.

This is important for families to remember as often the child with the label or illness gets all the attention and the other kids feel left out. I've seen this quite a lot and think its important to treat families as units of individuals but as a whole. When someone is ill it effects the whole family constellation.

So thanks for being there.

Hope to hear your thoughts soon.
Love and hugs,

Marsha

March 24, 1997

Reflections on Radiation...

We're back from Cincinnati - where we just
did a two day PATH with the Kentucky
Developmental Disabilities Council. They were not easy, but it
did "make a difference". We left exhausted – but charged up.
We needed that after last week.

"Last Week" was a week in purgatory, but the thermostat
was out of control and it felt like the warmer end of that waiting room a good deal of the time. We got back from
Yellowknife (on March 8) and charged into the first of what
turned out to be an interminable series of doctor appointments.
It was supposed to be simple – but... you know the rest – only
the details vary. In addition to a now very LONG list of doctors
who are "responsible" for different pieces of Marsha's
anatomy, we have now added a radiation oncologist and a
dermatologist – and all their attendant retinue. The tinge of
exhaustion is not hostility, because at the Princess Margaret
Hospital (yes another one) they have been extremely friendly,
supportive and generally functioning like it should. However,
we still had to "break in" another hospital. Happily Mount
Sinai Hospital, Toronto General Hospital and the Princess
Margaret Hospital are all physically linked – you don't even
have to go outdoors –   although you do need to start at the
beginning of the food chain each time.

All was going according to plan. We were trying to inject a
sense of urgency into the radiation planning. It took extensive
"engineering" to tease the system into quicker action. Dr. Paul
Levy after MANY calls, found the magic word – " *Money*".
It was not a "bribe." Rather, when Paul noticed that cries of

"urgent" went unheard through the white noise, he told us to say, "lots of money" to get people's attention. So we said, "We are self employed. If we cancel workshops – it costs us lots of **money**." The magic word my mother taught me was 'please'. This time, ears perked up and eyes focused when we said, "money". We enunciated our magic words and managed to get most of the actors doing their jobs on cue. Don't get us wrong. Money was not our agenda. Money was the "cue" to getting people's attention. No one was nasty or being a laggard. It was just that we couldn't "move it" until we said "money." All was going well... We finally got to the bowels of the Princess Margaret where there are 18 huge super high tech radiation machines. Marsha got "measured and tattooed," and ready for the treatment. But ... there is always a but! The next morning, following the tattoo, Marsha had a huge rash – precisely where they had marked. The breast surgeon we were seeing ("regular follow up visit") expressed fascination and dismay. We went to the Radiation Clinic (where we had been the day before) and gate crashed. They were really nice – and equally puzzled, having never seen this before. Could radiation proceed??? If it couldn't – our whole UK schedule was down the tubes... "Money, money, money" we whisper.

Go to Photography department and make pictures.

Do not pass go.

Go to biopsy dept. - still no $200.

Go to a Dermatologist "this afternoon". (We are scheduled for a workshop in Cincinnati in the morning)

[Money, money, money echoes are heard]. Princess Margaret can't do Skin in the afternoon. We page our doctor friend Yves, who finds his friend, a dermatologist - 2:00 p.m. Everyone looks. "Hmmmmmmmm."

Go to Cincinnati and watch it.....

Come back Monday.

Radiation delayed till Thursday...

UK still on.. Can we fit in 21 cooking days – and still make it on the plane at the month end? Radiation begins (we hope) on Thursday March 27.

None of this is about health. It's all about scheduling. Scheduling is an iatrogenic disease. It can cause heart burn and heart attacks. Waiting is hard. Doing things is better. So... we went to Cincinnati.

Our two days with the DD Council were great. A wonderful group of people – all committed, but in this case, without a shared vision. We worked on that – and the KDD Vision Quest made headway ending with the whole group linked in a circle of support. Equally important, a team was appointed to present the PATH to those who had not been present at the beginning of the Board meeting. No fuzzy first steps.

And now, we return to editing, and compiling *Inclusion News*, the Web Page, additions – and more, and more, and more. Lest we forget, our last "missive" was composed in Alaska – and sent from Yellowknife or Toronto. Thus, some of you may have missed the "energizer" that got us ready to endure the medical waiting week. Yellowknife was wonderful. (March 1-8). We stayed with our friends Ken and Margaret, who gave us space, wine, good food, warm hospitality, and space again. One of our learnings for us, on this particular journey, is that we need "space" – quiet time without agendas, people, and all those entrails. It isn't "personal" – against individuals, but rather a recognition that we need quiet time – some of the time. Part of the space was provided by nature's own spectacles – viewed from on the ice-road at night. The Northern Lights and the comet linked us to an eternal beauty in a way that can't be reached with e-mail – and for me that means high praise! In addition to providing space, Ken Woodley (the Superintendent of Yellowknife One School Board) hired us to work with YK1. He is a "high risk operator." We asked if we could "shoot a video" and he agreed. We brought our friend Jeff Dobbin from Toronto. We talked with Jeff about a metaphor for the film. When we agreed on "dog teams," Ken picked up the phone and hours later, we were out on the ice in the "baskets" behind a dog team – hearing the crackle of ice underneath at -35. We learned a lot about the "teamwork" and the "work" of building a dog team. Monday morning (March 3), 25 high school students were "sprung" to help plan a better future for their school. We spent a day working very hard to create a Path entitled "Creating Our Future."

We thought we were done. Then Ken, the seemly quiet superintendent who had been in the middle all day, explained that the System Administrative Team – all the Principals, Vice-Principals and senior administrators were going to be meeting for the next two days and doing the same thing. Would the students like to monitor the adults? A wave of hands surged forward almost crushing the poor man with enthusiasm. Five were chosen to see that the "student path" would be given a full and fair hearing, and that their voices would be heard first, and not second hand. Quite a day. All this was on video which we will (in time) edit. The next two days were the Yellowknife 1 Administrative Team PATH. It is a courageous leader that invites ALL the team into a room, with a video, and a group of high school student participants, to plan the future for the system. Ken Woodley did that. It worked. We got through. They created a "train" and got on board.

As we left Yellowknife, we felt that at least one school system had started on a new journey and was pulling out of the station, laying new track to "Create Our Future" – together. We hope the video will capture the excitement and the hard work to get the train moving. We'll keep you posted on "release dates." It will be a few months.

Some Reflections:

It seems like it's time to add a few of my own reflections to this sharing circle – where many of us are facing our nightmares and choosing to live life rather than die it. I won't bother with the pretense that cancer is a gift, or that you should try it because it will teach you so much. We all learn. But this has a mound of garbage that comes with it, and I certainly wouldn't choose it. However, although it isn't easy, when I look at our calendar for the past two months, we have actually only postponed one event, and we managed to do some extraordinary work in Winnipeg, Anchorage, Yellowknife, Cincinnati – and more. We have not been stopped. Some would see this schedule as exhausting. For us, the schedule is our "energizer". Waiting, without control is the debilitator. So we have endeavoured to "take control", or at least engineer the illusion of control, for some small pieces of this period. It keeps us sane and healthier.

Since many friends and readers seem to be using this "dialogue in hyper space" as a way of exploring their own issues, I want to add some of my learning's so far:

First, and without reservation – **DO NOT DO IT ALONE!** There is all kind of historical evidence, and modern medical research that confirms that those who are connected are healthier and do better – period. In the 'Head Game' of Cancer this is reaffirmed daily. Let me explain some of the ways.

289

Dream Catchers and Dolphins

Marsha and I are a good couple. Some of you might consider this an understatement – but we live, love and work together almost 24 hours a day, and we even like being with one another the vast majority of that time. We don't fight, even though being human we have irritable moments. My point is that our relationship in isolation is very solid, but it would have been strained to breaking – if we were doing this alone. Examples make the point. In crisis, often Marsha needs to "explode with words" – and I (a different style) become very quiet. Under normal circumstances, this is not an issue. But if Marsha didn't have Paul, and Victoria, and Cathy and ... some of her chosen "listeners" IN ADDITION to me, I would be a wreck. I can't be Marsha's therapist, and her husband/lover/co-worker. So, by consciously creating "listening" partners, Marsha cleared a space in our life for us to just be us – and not be "doing cancer" every minute of every day. It allows us to get on with life.

I also have my "listeners". They are different than Marsha's, because I am different. Neil is one; and Neil and I "do lunch". His partner of many years recently died of AIDS. Neil allows me to think the unthinkable, set it aside, and then get back on track. For me, life without Marsha is unthinkable. I don't want to think about it. I can't think about it. It is a painful waste of time – for me. But the truth is that I have a gnawing terror... it creeps up on me here and there. I play all the little head games "Why couldn't it be me...??", but it isn't. With Neil, little is said, but my nightmares are acknowledged, noted, and then carefully packed away in the fervent hope that I will never have to face them. Then, having faced my greatest fear – I go on.

Some of the most frustrating times are very mundane. My

perception is that in a full blown crisis, I can get focused and do what needs to be done. But this cell disease is a mean enemy. Its most vicious trait is the exhaustion of "endless uncertainty." If we could just "have an answer about what to do," and know that if we did 'x' for 12 months twice a day for 2 hours – it would be done. But cell disease isn't like that. It is like a virus that transforms certainty into uncertainty. It has a voracious appetite which insidiously gnaws away every day. Very seldom does it take big bites. Rather, it wears you down. You go for a test, and correctly but insidiously, there is another "shadow," a swelling, a pimple. They are all "nothing," but "under the circumstances, we'll check it out.." Then one waits. The results are usually inconclusive, and the "strategy" is to monitor "it" for a year or two. All this is correct medically, but it feeds into the "Big Lie Propaganda Strategy" of cell disease. It just wears you down. It is that eternal drip, drip, drip which means nothing – and erodes your sanity. No single visit to a doctor is particularly traumatic, but the daily, regular reminder that you are vulnerable is debilitating. The iatrogenic impact of cancer care is enormously corrosive. I am not criticizing some of the truly remarkable medical services that have kept us alive, but noting the enormous power of the medical system to sap the energy for life with endless testing, waiting, more testing, and endless waiting...

All this is balanced by the fact that even with the enormous stresses on the Canadian Medicare system right now, it is still working. We are getting excellent medical care. Without it we would be dead. We appreciate it. And, simultaneously, this is hard to live with. The stress points are not the obvious ones like surgery and major interventions. Those are stressful, but as human beings, we can create an adrenaline surge to get through those days. The hard bits are coming to terms with living with interminable daily uncertainty. It's the 'little" annoyances that chip away at your confidence, your energy, your will to live. Which is why I come back to my central learning. Do not do it alone. You won't make it.

As much as all this applies to a crisis in cell disease, which many of us will encounter personally, it is equally about the long haul to build a better world, where we just learn to live with one another. It is important to pass the right laws and policies, but simultaneously, the hard work is the daily regimen, within our own families, with our neighbours, with people we like – and more important, people we don't like. It is the daily grind of difficulties where change takes place.

A variant on this theme of '*don't do it alone*' – is my deeper understanding that cell disease (or any other crisis) is not the exclusive turf of one person. Marsha has the cell disease in her body, but WE are living with cancer. It is a family affair. Too often, we have the illusion that the person at the centre of an issue is the only one in need of support. Not true. When a crisis strikes, it hits the whole "unit". We are doing well on this front, but it is frightening to see the disguised terror and loneliness as one looks at people in the cancer waiting rooms. Some are there alone!!! And some of the partners and friends are so drawn and fearful and so alone. We can't fix all of that, but we can do what each of us can do – "one starfish" at a time - and it does make a difference to that starfish – every time.

I have been exploring the nightmare I choose to contain, most of the time. This is not where I spend most of my energy because I have faced my nightmare – and I can set it aside. I don't know what I will do if Marsha..... But the truth is, none of us do, and I choose not to explore that un-mappable chasm. IF that day comes, I will deal with it. In the meantime, I intend to re-energize my life with our work, because we think we have learned some things that can help others. We have an obligation to do that and do it every day – just in case a stray bus interferes with our video production schedule.

So my strategy for coping is work and celebration. We have reviewed our schedule and asked the questions like, "If we only had six months to live, what would we do?" Our answer is, "What we are doing." We added an extra week of scuba diving at Christmas. That was so good. We signed on for a Pacific Diving exploration near the Queen Charlotte Islands in August. We are being more conscious about rest. We MUST take care of ourselves and not get run down. We are only doing things that we think "make a difference." We are more focused. We choose to not invest time in whining – either generating or listening to it. On the other hand, we have and are making time for those who are genuinely struggling with the chaos and complexity of change. For us, travel works. As much as Toronto is a wonderful place and our house is warm and welcoming, it has two engrained strains. Firstly, it is our office which generates its own pressures – mostly good. Secondly, Toronto has all our hospitals, which are wonderful for taking such good care, and simultaneously – a constant reminder of our vulnerability. So, some travel is good, but we are building in rest periods. We cannot risk getting too over-tired – or sick. That would be "giving in" to the disease.

We are doing the best we know how. The waves of support - by e-mail, letters, cards, et al, are humbling – and are absolutely essential for our energy renewal. It is not incidental – it is primary. It wouldn't be for everyone. For us it works. I might not have done it, but Marsha did, and I'm glad. Perhaps one of the most powerful forces of renewal is some of the stories some of you have told us. Not one, or two, but a dozen or more stories have already emerged where our letters were shared. People who had been avoiding a test or people who were reluctant to ask have "taken charge" – they are choosing to be active participants in their own path to full health. We all know that we don't "control" all the elements, but we can be full participants in building our own futures. Hearing those stories means this is working.

I do not suggest that this is the only, or the right way – but it is working for me.

We begin the radiation on Thursday (27th). We will have a small reflective time just before we go to the "big burn." We were privileged on our recent visit to Winnipeg to visit with Mae Louise Campbell – an aboriginal friend and artist. She told us the story of the Clan Mothers – in particularly, the 'Healer of the Healers'. She had created an exquisite clay figurine, clad in deerhide and beads, which now resides as the centre piece of our living room. Marsha phoned Mae Louise and asked if she had a drum – perhaps with turtles. Mae Louise said she would make one. It just arrived. It will drum us into this next phase of the struggle. The phone just intoned another message of support "storming the heavens". We are doing that. Perhaps the most fitting closing to this note are Mae Louise's instructions that come with my drum. They are life instructions with centuries of wisdom from the elders. We can all learn from her wisdom.

"To Jack: This drum will be your friend. Use it wisely with Respect. Know it will calm you when you are anxious or worried; help you to relieve your anger; help to vibrate your energy to the universe when you pray or meditate; celebrate with you when you are happy and joyous. It is a healing companion to you and your loved ones always.

Enjoy and Respect it. Your sister, Mae Louise." "Turtle
Drum: This drum represents our Earth Mother and All Our
Relations. The Turtle situated in the Centre is Turtle
Island or Mother Earth. I have painted each one of her legs
one of the four colours which are part of our Medicine
Wheel. They tell us there are four Nations and Four
Seasons. The thirteen spaces on the Turtles' back connect
us to the 13 Moon cycles and the Universe. The Red line
shows we are all brothers and sisters on Turtle Island. The
symbols around Turtle represent all our relations – Sky
Nation, Thunder and Lightening, Plant People, Water and
Water Creatures, Feathered Relations, Four Legged Animals. Your Drum is your personal friend. It represents the
heart beat of Mother Earth. When you use it the vibrations
travel into the Universe to All our Relations – to Mother
Earth, to Creator, Connecting you to All."

That is a perfect Gift.

And Thursday morning, we will vibrate with all of you -
with the universe – as we prepare to focus the healing energies
of our collective spirits – and the laser focus of the radiation so
we can continue our work together.

Jack

Dreamcatchers and Dolphins

March 30, 1997

Easter and Passover Greetings

Dear Friends and Support Network,

Well we did it! The radiation began and we feel relieved. It is the "not knowing", the "unknown," that is so scary. We want to go to England and Scotland in May to work and play. That means we need the 21 radiation days to start now. The doctors are also letting me go to Connecticut to work as a break in the middle of the radiation. Hurrah! Let's de-mystify the radiation. It is localized to the right breast. It takes about 2 minutes (plus setup and waiting). It does not hurt. We have chosen to see this as a "break" in our work day – from office stuff and *Inclusion News*. We choose not to victimize or medicalize our lives. I REFUSE to be defined as sick. I am healthy and dealing with living with cancer. We thank everyone for their respectful support, and for balancing our need for support with our need for space. I am staying far away from people who see me as sick or who want to medicalize my life. Equally dangerous are those who are in need of help and don't know it. Protect me from those who want to help, when they need to listen to "first things first" and reach out for personal help before harming others.

A local circle of friends visits, laughs, cries, and eats together; stays away when necessary, and comes close when needed. We are working all the time (as usual). Life is continuing and as Paul Levy says, we are "not only surviving but thriving." Work, for us, is life, and life is work. There is no major distinction. That is rare and we are grateful for this way of living.

An international circle of friends is there, plus a wider

network of support is there, with words, prayers, thoughts, cards, etc. Very few have crossed the line; and even then that's OK, as long as we don't get sucked into other people's agendas. Quite frankly, we just don't have the energy for anything that is not healthy and moving in a progressive direction. Negative energy will find other outlets for itself. It just needs to stay away from our door. As Shafik says, if this all means that at times you won't be so "nice", so be it. "Be at one with yourself" he advises. The man speaks right to my gut. He always offers his "cool runnings" (that means peace be your journey.) And I listen and I learn.

We just finished reading David Schwartz's new book *Who Cares, Rediscovering Community*, (Westview Press, Boulder, Co.) It is great. We highly recommend it. This analysis also validates us in the struggle we are currently living. David manages to capture the paradoxes of these times without blaming the people directly involved in the system. It is hard, in the middle of a crisis, not to blame individuals who are caught in a web of insanity themselves. The lesson for us is to use the traditional services as needed, but not expect them to take the place of the real caring that comes from friends – near and far. To attempt to make the medical system "CARE" would be a waste of energy and effort. And even writing this is a paradox, as many of our doctors have been wonderful. But they cannot ever replace Jack or Cathy, or Rose, or Victoria, or John or .... Our mistake, as a culture, has been to allow ourselves to be deluded into the illusion that systems of any kind could re-place/provide the love and care of friends and family. Systems can supplement – but not replace fundamental relationships.

I keep feeling I "should" say something profound. But just

living every day is profound. Just walking, just working, just reading is profound. Just doing one good thing every day is profound. I am still overcome with fear at times. I am overwhelmed with the love from Jack and those around us. Around us includes the gang in Nottingham, the crew in Yellowknife, and friends all over the world. For us, community is a community of interest and indeed a community of kindred spirits. It is both local and international for us.

I think e-mail is the modern day form of letter writing; a way of connecting families together. For me, writing has always been the safest way of communicating. Being from New York City, where everyone has thirty simultaneous conversations in search of a topic, I always felt a need to be heard in a different way. Ever since I met Jack, I have written to him as it gave me a chance to speak my heart in a way I couldn't in talking. It gave him a chance to respond in his own time and his own way. So it is with all of you out there who are responding in your own unique and wonderful ways to us.

Everything I am reading these days seems to be coming down to the same critical points. In a monograph on educational change, Michael Fullan, a major academic writer on educational change writes: "...all change produces the fear of the unknown, ambivalence and anxiety – we begin to see what has to be done. Helping ourselves and other people better manage the upsetting feelings of change is the healthiest thing we can do."

Goleman, (author of *Emotional Intelligence*), provides yet a another starting point in the same vein: "Studies done over two decades, involving more than 37,000 people, show that social isolation (the sense that you have nobody with whom you can share your private feelings, have close contact) doubles the chances of sickness or death."

We have to learn to take care of each other. It is healthier, and in a time when we control so little, we can choose to build stronger relationships – to reach out to one another.

In our wonderful walks and talks, my walking buddy, Victoria, and I explore the depths of the wounded healer. We both admit to our own deep wounds as a first step; as a starting place to who we really are. She has had much experience with Alcoholics Anonymous and Jungian therapy. I learn much from our musings. We walk and we muse. I often cry. She listens. She was there when my mother was very ill many years ago. She disappeared for awhile and has resurfaced as a guardian angel. The angel part is the listening. And I listen back. She is a treasure in my life.

Victoria and I are exploring the danger of people in the 'helping professions' who can't help themselves. People who have empty circles and attempt to assist others to build circles are dangerous to themselves and others. I have also explored this with my friend, mentor and therapist Paul Levy. We all feel that helpers have to step out of the role of helper and become people first. The helpers must personally reach out for help. We expect people with disabilities to get up in public and tell their dreams, stories, nightmares – yet we never would be able or willing to do it. That is the paradox. I have felt this contradiction for years, but I thought I had to be "certified" as a psychologist, psychiatrist, etc. to write about "that". It was OK for me to write about inclusion, tools for change, etc., but what right did I have to tackle the big stuff like living?

Dream Catchers and Dolphins

Well I am tackling it. It is this big stuff that keeps me alive. It is the crap that takes me under. For example, a friend was worrying whether she was bothering us as she was struggling with real problems in her life. She was real, and beautiful, and in pain. It was energizing. It is like when I am in terrific fear and anguish and I call Shafik. He tells me he loves me like this and how wonderful I am. I tell him I hate him (laughing) and we carry on. It is the game playing, the manipulating, the secrets and lies that drive me crazy. Dealing with real pain, of a real friend in my real kitchen, is what life is all about.

Again the paradox. You can't do this with everyone. Many want to come into our circle when they need to build their own. Judith Snow has been amazing in this respect. Knowing how much energy we are investing on survival, and knowing how much energy she needs to survive daily, Judith has been building and adding to her own circle. She is moving again soon. We support her, but have not been involved as we would have been in the past. Has this eroded our friendship? No. Indeed, it has opened a new door. A more grounded door. A deeper door. Judith has given us the space we needed, and in so doing has added to her life. We are still there, but in a new and even deeper way.

And then there is us letting new flowers bloom. Our new flowers live across the street. They are 5 children who I love. I watch them. I wonder at their parents. I don't invade or intrude, but invite when appropriate. They will be with us for a very small Seder that I am making – just for them. It will be a teaching Seder for these five adopted grandchildren. The tribe increases slowly but surely, step by step. One night in Yellowknife, we were privileged to see the aurora borealis. It was magic in the sky. Science can explain it. Seeing it was another magical moment in life. We stood with a new friend, which made it even more intense. It was 40 below zero. We knew we were alive and well. We have no desire to stop this life ride we are on. We are learning to balance the need to rest and the need for work. I just cannot take unnecessary stress as there is much day-to-day stuff I must do to survive. I have no desire to run away or to "retire". That is not a word in our vocabulary. We just want to build this community of yearners for a better world, step by step. It is not easy, but it is right.

Often people say to us, "You are so strong." We say, "We are so human." It is time to "Tell the whole truth." The whole truth is that dealing with cancer, divorce, loss or change is just plain hard. There are days I have trouble getting out of bed. There are wells of tears in me. I wish that I didn't have to go to the hospital every day for radiation. I wish I didn't have this disease. Paradoxically, I am so grateful to live in Toronto where I can get treatment. I am so grateful I live across the street from Cathy. I am so grateful for Rose and Barbara and Judith; and I am most of all so grateful for Jack. That is the whole truth.

Tears flow even as I write this. I am so tired of judging myself. I am listening to Kenny G and not Beethoven and that's OK. I love to read John McKnight, David Schwartz, O'Brien, Hardial Bains, and as well mystery books and cookbooks. I am in pain listening to those who work with vulnerable people not admitting to their own humanity. I weep for women attempting to change for men who themselves need to change. I weep for men attempting to change for women who themselves need to change. And I laugh with 'tickle-me' Elmo at the utter simplicity of it all. There is help at hand – if we reach out and ask one another for human kindness and care. If I cannot reach out, I cannot ask anyone else to. So I did reach out, and I continue to do so.   The richness of the "return" is incredible. A book is being born. A dialogue is being created.

We have turned another corner. It has not been easy. And yet in the middle of this crisis we made a video in Yellowknife that will make an impact on people's lives; we rode in a dog sled. We flew over icy blue glaciers in Alaska. We worked. We laughed. We cried. We lived!

Call your own circles and stay part of ours, each in your own unique way. Many of you seem to be hearing this. That's great. We can't do it alone. These days being alone in crisis is truly dangerous. It is the time for connections.

I do not, nor will we romanticize this struggle, this journey. It is rough. But as Shafik always says, a heart monitor is up and down. A flat line is death."

This is the weekend of the bi-annual Tuhoe festival in New Zealand. We can feel the music and the stomping intensity of feet in the 'haka' performed by the children and adults of the tribe which generously adopted us – and we them.

We too are part of a large international tribe of people joined by common values and striving and longing for connection, belonging and community. Inclusion is really a wonderful thing, a marvellous work and a marvellous word. It means embracing one another.

So whether you celebrate Easter, Passover, or the coming Spring, we embrace you and wish you health and well being for you and your circles.

Much Love,

Marsha

Dreamcatchers and Dolphins

Dear Marsha and Jack:

Thank you for your greetings. Here on All Fool's Day, spring is coming to the prairies. I saw my first flock of geese yesterday, just as Environment Canada predicted. The snow is melting. Marvellously, the grass is already greening up underneath the receding snow. In one corner of my garden, the red tips of the first branches of peonies are showing. Later this week, I will shovel out the snow from around my apple tree, where the drifts were high; remove the blanket of leaves, that I put in the fall, from around the base of the trunk; and wait for the dozens of daffodils that will bloom there.

Spring has always been my favourite time of year, probably because my birthday is in May. Living on the prairies (as Jack knows full well), spring can be a fast and violent time. This year, while we stop to appreciate the thaw, we count on our hands the inches of snow melted (and going into the ground) versus that which is dehydrated (into the air)... But it seems to me that this is always the way: Two sides to every coin – a different interpretation, coming or going.

We are all travellers in our own day and time. The two of you are viewing things from one spot. As it is (or should be with all travellers), it is good to get your news (views) relayed back to the rest of us.

Keep writing and sending us letters from your vantage point. In this way, we can begin to learn more about each other and ourselves.

Lots of love, *Zana L.*

Marsha Forest & Jack Pearpoint

April 19, 1997

April Showers

Dear Friends,

We just got back from a wonderful and reflective workshop in Connecticut. Organized by Communitas (George Ducharme, Pat Beeman and Ernie Pancsofar) this was held at the beautiful Mercy Centre, on Long Island Sound. The setting is a retreat centre, run by nuns, and the place lends itself to learning and reflection. There were 65 participants and in four days they worked very diligently on the "tools for change" we are sharing around the globe.

The group was diverse with a mix of professionals, families, consumers of services, etc. We find these are always the best groups as the cross pollination, across disciplines, always adds to the learning. We now look forward to our trip to Scotland and England at beginning of May.

The radiation treatments are going well and I am not having many side effects. The hospital is well organized and gets me in and out within a half hour. This is a blessing. We wrote a thank you letter praising the doctors and nurses on this unit for their ability to be sensitive and well organized. It is stressful enough going into the doors of the hospital, let alone having to wait for hours.

Life for me these days can be summed up in the word "paradox." I am fine and not fine. I am healthy and not perfectly healthy. I am strong. I am vulnerable. I am happy. I am sad. I

305

am energetic. I am tired. The problem for me lies in thinking that I "should" be fine or happy all the time. These are echoes of my past telling me I must be "superwoman" to be loved. I know these voices aren't really there and aren't really real, but they exert enormous pressure. I am dealing with them. I am learning as in the words of Alice Walker, "I don't have to be perfect to be loved, indeed nobody is." And I am feeling loved for being and living the paradox. For just being me.

What would I tell anyone else in my situation? What words would I share? I would of course say, "You have experienced so much stress and trauma – take it easy, take care of yourself, rest, eat well, do what it takes." I am learning to take my own advice. It is not easy, but I can't stand watching people who give advice not taking it themselves. Therefore I am resting more, eating well, taking more bubble baths, and even taking a nap when I want to. This has not been easy. At the beginning of the radiation treatments I went into the massive hyper superwoman role. I'd prove I was strong and tough. I was shopping and cooking and flying around to prove I was OK. This of course is when I drive Jack and myself totally crazy.

But we caught the "syndrome" fast and I followed those wonderful Scuba Rules: "Stop. Breathe. Think. Act." I stopped trying to be "superwoman" and lo and behold I still did what I needed to do and I also didn't drive myself, Jack, or anyone else around me nuts in the process.

All I can say is that we are doing the very best we can do. There is not much more we can do. The rest is out of our hands. We live and we hope for the best, just like the rest of you who are reading this. I often wish I could go back and visit the me (Marsha) of July 1995 before the major surgery. But that me was then and this me is now. My values and beliefs haven't changed. I am as passionate as ever about creating a more just and fair world for ALL! But inside of me there have been changes. Changes that are inevitable. The growth as we know is optional and I have chosen to grow and learn from all of this. What other choice is there?

I value quiet time and comfort more. I can't and won't tolerate the petty stupid stuff. I treasure the work we do and the friends we have. I appreciate my relationship with Jack even more (if that's possible) and I am learning to really live one day at a time to the fullest. We have no desire to retire, to run away, or to change the general direction of our lives. Doing less at times is doing more, as I am learning daily. I also see, more than ever, the pain and suffering around me, as well as the joy and celebration. This I think is making me more balanced and yet less happy. But I am not looking for happiness, I am more interested in meaning and making a difference. Happy comes as well, and when it does it comes in even more beautiful colours than ever before.

Because my medical stuff is so complex, I find myself wanting to simplify things. My friend, Paul, made an analogy to me living in a little European village. I go to my bakery, shop in the wonderful new market nearby, run over and see my friend and her children, call friends for the local chatter, cook, eat and read. I venture out into the world to do my work and then fly home to the little village which is home and hearth. I like that. I love our home. It is, as Dave Hollands said, "like a comfortable old sweater." We look forward to opening our home to some of you who will be here for the Summer Institute.

Dream Catchers and Dolphins

I am full of energy and yet very tired at the same time. I am tired of being so scared and tired of worrying. I often wish my very nature was different. But I am who I am and I am finally learning to live with that. I can and am working hard to tame the tiger of fear for it is energy draining and consuming. It is there however, so I can say hello to it, give it some time each day, and then let it go and get on with the day. It is because I love life so much that I still fear illness and death and yet they are facts of life. Again the paradox. So as Paul says I am doing pretty well this month, given that I am dealing with: (1) radiation everyday; (2) a new drug called Tamoxifin for prevention of cancer; and (3) massive doses of fear and anxiety. I laugh and I cry. I work and I play. There is so much to do and I often wish I didn't have to bother so much about myself. But at this point in my life I do. Bothering about myself means I may survive all this – to keep on being part of the movement to make this world a better place. I am one of the fortunate ones. I am determined to fight even harder so that everyone can get the quality of care I am getting. No one should have to pay a cent for medical treatment. It is criminal that poor women die simply because they are poor and can't afford treatments that can, and do, save lives. The technology is there. It must serve everyone, not just a slice of the society. Not just those with education and with money. All must mean all!

The politics of this are more clear than ever for me. Are people entitled to health, education, a livelihood and a decent life? Or are they not? Do some rate care, while others are defined as less than worthy? These are really the naked questions of the day. In Canada we are still fortunate to have universal health care, but that is eroding quickly. We must fight to preserve the rights we have.

My dear friend, Nathan Gilbert, just sent me the notes of a talk Jonathan Kozol gave at a foundation meeting he attended. Kozol's newest book *Amazing Grace* describes the tragedy and triumph of one of the poorest sections of the United States (the South Bronx) – a place in which my family used to live when I was a child. Now it is a ghetto for the poor African American families. Kozol asks if we will tolerate this increasing ghettoization of the society.

Kozol doesn't romanticize the poverty, but he sees (as we saw in the Maori communities in New Zealand) the incredible strength of the people, particularly the grandmothers and the youth. I am going out immediately to buy the book.

Thus in a sense, I see my own personal crisis mirroring the political crisis around me. I can either drop out, despair, moan and groan, get cynical and be passive - or - I can face the reality and get fully engaged in the battle to save my own life and make this a better world for the youth of the future. I choose the latter.

I get impatient with people (in our own network) who see "inclusion" as a narrow little issue rather than the big issue it really is. How can we "include" some little child with a disability when we don't yet see that all human beings have value. We overheard a horrible conversation, by two men on the plane, which sums up one side of the coin. They were arrogantly discussing how "nobody is entitled to anything unless they work to deserve it." Mean and simple.

Dream Catchers and Dolphins

Kozol describes these men and women as a team who don't fight with each other, who are loyal to one another and who are the "smartest, meanest, most malicious, most consummately evil people I have ever run into." This describes the people in political positions in both Canada and the USA. (many other places too).

Our team (i.e. the "good caring folks") needs to stop bickering over the little stuff and unite on the big issues of the day. The big issues, for many people these days, include the very right to life itself. When education and medical care become only the venue for the rich and powerful, we have dangerous times indeed. This is a time for careful vigilance and all sided real thinking. There are no simplistic answers. I believe there are masses of good people, in small groups everywhere, who need to connect and talk to one another. E-mail is one channel to open the door to real dialogue.

So that's where I'm at. I am taking care of myself and at the same time reflecting deeply into the role I will continue to play to make this world better for all of us. If there is meaning in my own healing, it is to continue to write, and speak out and be part of a movement for real democracy and human rights.

Jack and I leave for England on May 1, 1997 - exactly 21 years since we met on the plane going to China in 1976. There have been lots of changes in the world since then and lots of changes in us. One thing hasn't changed - our commitment to each other and to being part of changing the world.

I'll write again from Europe. We hope this letter finds you all well and struggling each in his/her unique way to bring music, laughter and life into your own communities and circles.

Keep in touch. We treasure your communications with us.

Much love,

Marsha

And a word from Jack:

Our niece and nephew arrive Wednesday for a blast of Toronto. That will keep us busy. Marsha finishes radiation Friday. Hurraaahhhh! We have a two day workshop with the Board of Laidlaw Foundation – and then on May 2 - we will materialize in Glasgow – beginning a month in Scotland and England. Between then and now there is much to do – and never enough time. This is the way it should be. We saw daffodils in the raw in Connecticut – and here in Toronto – raw is still operative. The sun is warm – but it is not t-shirt weather. Hale-Bopp?? the comet was clear above Toronto last night so we all gathered in the street with the Hollands and tried to understand what 130,000,000 miles away looks like. Love life and enjoy every day. Have a wonderful spring.

Jack

Dreamcatchers and Dolphins

April 26, 1997

Spring

Dear John,

Well 21 radiation treatments done and tonight I bought a good bottle of French champagne to celebrate. Cathy and Dave will come over and we will celebrate life.

If I wrote you at various times in a day you'd get a different mood. I am OK and I am not OK. I am truly paradoxical. I have not yet reintegrated into a new whole. All these blows have knocked me out a bit and yes I am more humble, vulnerable etc and also I hate all this medical stuff like you wouldn't believe. Going to that hospital every day was totally weird. I kept saying, What am I doing here? I am a healthy person. I am a hiker, a mountain climber. Why am I here?

Well in reality I was there because I have breast cancer and I am being treated so it won't comeback. It is a miracle I am here. It is a miracle it was caught. Am I OK?

Why is my appetite so crazy? Why do I get tired earlier? Why me?

I know...Why not me and all that but still at times I get really MAD. I hate this. I didn't write this script. And then I drop that conversation and go on. What else is there to do? I will not play the sick role. I simply will not. Yes I will rest. Yes I need solitude and I can't deal with extra stress. and Yes tonight I will drink a good bottle of French champagne with

312

Jack and Cathy and Dave and celebrate getting through 21 days of radiation.

It is a lot to take and you are one of the lucky few that get to see the real let the mucous flow side. I can't wait to get on the plane to Scotland. If the plane flew around the world I'd be happy to sit and read and reflect and watch the clouds roll by. I am to deeply tired. Not sleepy but weary. I feel my body has been assaulted and needs to heal. I love feeling cozy and sleeping with and next to Jack. I, as Shafik said in the tape, need to feel warm and comfortable more.

Baths and good beds and good food and good friends.

PS. We did an amazing Seder with Cathy and I put together our own personalized Haggadah and Seder service. It was wonderful. May we celebrate Chanukah and Passover with them each year!

That's all for now.

Much love.

Marsha

Dreamcatchers and Dolphins

July 15, 1997

Summer Update and the Summer Institute

Dear Friends,

Two years ago on July 28, 1995, I was diagnosed with Ovarian Cancer and went into major surgery August 4. Chemo followed. Fear and anxiety hit! We got through it. I lost my hair, but never my hope. And Jack was there – heart and soul. Healing.

In January 1997, was diagnosed with very early but serious breast cancer. Surgery again. Radiation and then a dream trip to England and that magic week-end in Paris.

We survived. IF IT DOESN'T KILL YOU IT MAKES YOU STRONGER. We are stronger. We are also wiser, more humble and very focused. We have no desire to run away or retire. We just want to carry on. Our life is rich, full, and deeply filled with our work, our play, our circle.

On July 28th we will fly to Anchorage to work and play. We have built in time to sail and fly in Alaska. Then we go to British Columbia for an adventure scuba diving trip in cold Pacific waters. It should be beautiful boating up the coast and seeing eagles, whales and dolphins, and the beauty of the earth. How lucky we are! At the end of August we do a 4 day workshop in Cranbrook, B.C. and head home Aug. 31. I will be 55 and alive (Aug. 10, 1997). As I write this, tears spill for each day and each year is so very precious.

314

I still do not see cancer as a "gift" but rather as a given. And given that's what we got given, our view is to live life even more to the fullest. Each of us chooses his/her own PATH. Ours is to serve, work and live till we drop.

I have learned (not liked) that life includes life and death, health and sickness, joy and sorrow, the whole ball park. I am not willing to spend much time on petty "stuff" or to be with "petty and small minded people." We are targeting work that we feel will really make a difference and we are learning to say "no" and "yes" to the right things for us to do.

For us, being together is healthy and healing. The vulnerability of this love is very intense and really scares me, for I don't think I could make it without Jack's steadfast loyalty and love. But that is also a given of how it is and who we are.

And then the Toronto Summer Institute 97... Surrounded by you all out there and a hard core of devoted and caring friends we have come through these two years able to create a piece of art called the Summer Institute. It was amazing. We created a true community of learning. We created a new format that transformed most everyone there. We will be writing more about that soon. Jack gave it an A plus and Te Ripowai said it was "magic." We will all do it again July 4-10, 1998 and 1999.

And so as I face the joy of being alive at 55, I thank everyone who has travelled this PATH with us. I am full of hope and vitality and also still carry much fear and anxiety which I acknowledge is part of me and this journey. There are days I am still overcome with fear and tears. That is OK. That is me. I cry, I laugh, I do it all!

Dream Catchers and Dolphins

We are really proud of the newest *Inclusion News*. It is a small book (32 pages) and has amazing articles by Judith, McKnight, Shafik, O'Brien, Hingsburger, Strully, us, and many others. We can't wait to hear your reactions to it. Let us know. We think this issue truly captures and reflects the depth and breadth of the deep meaning of inclusion.

I feel like I "should" say something wise or profound but the words that come to my mind are simply "thank you." Thank you and have a great summer. I need time to be on the water this summer. In the Pacific ocean I shall look at the stars each night and say "thank you.." thank you for each day. That is really the only guarantee – each day. I have found the only answer that I can find, and it is that the only answer to life is to live it.

We hope to hear from you and look forward to living and learning with all of you for the years to come.

Much love and peace,

Marsha and Jack

* Photo's of the **Grand Exalted Pooh-Bah** officiating at the opening of *Inclusion News* are featured on the web page.... do visit and enjoy. We may be 'off line' a fair bit this month - but the mail will get through, and we will do a Summer Institute review – when we have recovered and had a rest.

Jack

Afterword

Being a Web of Support

John O'Brien

The e-mail collected in this book can be read in two directions: more dramatically - and most importantly - as a chronicle of Marsha and Jack's quest for a way to live with two visitations of cancer, and secondly, more reflectively, as a sort of inventory of ways people can offer long-distance support to someone they care for. The first reading traces the path of respected members of a widely extended community of workers for social justice as they confront life and death with honesty, openness, vulnerability, courage, forthrightness and discipline and thereby take further steps toward becoming their community's elders. The second identifies some ways a community bereft of traditional ways can assist in the emergence of its elders.

In Marsha and Jack's summary e-mail updates, we read about the life-affirming activities of people who are physically and emotionally close enough to share walks and conversations, keep vigils that hospital workers will not easily forget, offer foot massages, bring chicken soup and jello and spaghetti, witness and comfort and confront Marsha's tears of fear and frustration and anger, listen to Jack face the unthinkable possibility of life without Marsha. These people, this circle of friends who live close by, had little need to get their news of Marsha and

317

Afterword

Jack from e-mail; they usually passed the news as friends and neighbors always have, from one's voice to another's ear.

However, in the e-mails collected here, we read a selection of the messages that trace an *extended* web of support across the distance between Calgary and Bristol and Sacramento and Nottingham and Philadelphia and Syracuse and Wellington and Lithonia and Yellowknife and Forest Grove. Some messages also cross personal distance as people reach out in messages that remind Marsha and Jack of the impact of attending one of their workshops. Some people move between physical presence and e-mail, but during the weeks and weeks of difficult times, most of the people in this web are present only as readers and senders of messages.

We have Marsha and Jack's clear and repeated statements that receiving these messages and composing responses to them were a help, and I want to read them in a way that highlights the different ways that people used this novel technology to express their care. My interest is more in the expression of care than in the technology. Most of what people did by e-mail could have been done with pen and paper. What would have been missing would have been the sense of belonging to the web that was generated by receiving the occasional broadcast e-mails from Jack and Marsha which make up much of the correspondence you have just read.

I hope that this reading complements rather than detracts

from the main messages of the book, which come from reading it as the story of Marsha and Jack's quest for health in the presence of cell disease (as they come to call it). Marsha's summary e-mails and commentary make these messages especially clear. For me, they could be summed up in seven challenging points. When visited by serious disease…

- Actively reach out to both your close and extended circles of relationships in order to look after your health and find physicians and nurses that you can trust to deal with the disease. This way you don't have to count on home remedies for complex diseases, and you don't have to count on technically engrossed doctors for the daily work of care, and you don't have to choose between these two essential aspects of living fully with life-threatening, misery-making illness .

- Strive to find, and regain when you lose, an understanding of yourself as a whole person with a disease; do not slip into seeing yourself or allowing others to see you as no more than the embodiment of a sickness.

- Cultivate the sensitivity to move away from what poisons you and drives you toward becoming an embodied illness and move toward what nurtures you and expresses your whole self, including the expression of whatever meaning might come to you from suffering the disease itself.

Afterword

- Act on the recognition that disease affects not only your spirit, mind, and body but also the spirit, mind, and body of your intimates.
- Help the people you choose to support you by letting them know as clearly as you can, as often as you need to, what works for you and what does not help and by reciprocating as you are able.
- Know that building and maintaining circles and webs of support for ourselves is the work of a lifetime; it's never too early to start building the connections that allow for the flow of caring and it's never too late to reach out.

Another look

Once the book's exposition of these essential messages is absorbed, it seems worth focusing a bit on the way people contributed to Marsha and Jack's extended web of support. There are two reasons I want to do this. First, because it is possible that some people might misread this book as a sort of advertisement for the healing powers of seeking some kind of general emotional support on-line. It is not that at all, and pausing to notice how what this book records differs from what some people enthusiastically call virtual community could make the difference between joining a buzz for the benefits of "e-support" and understanding e-mail as one more medium for expressing our concern for people we already know and care about. Some sobriety about understanding this difference falls in line with an item from the edition of The American Psychological Association's *Monitor* (*29*:9) that arrived while I was writing this. It reports a finding unexpected by the investigators in a two-year study of 169 adults who conduct a part of their social life over the internet: more use of e-mail and internet chat correlates with a loss of social contact, a decrease in the size of these people's social circles, and a rise in their symptoms of depression. Direct expression of care, with people close enough to smell and touch matters more to both people's well-being than all the e-mail in the world. But e-mail can remind us of our belonging and thus reinforce it.

Second, I want to think about this because I believe that some other people join me in the predicament of being distant neighbors and dispersed friends. We find people who come to matter to us through a pattern of attending the same events and working together on projects of mutual concern both in person and at a distance. Most of 160 people who shared this e-mail support web found Marsha and Jack through some aspect of their lifelong work for social justice. If neighbors are those who live close enough to know and share some life with, then a number of the contributors to this book live the oxymoron of being distant neighbors. Distant neighbors can't replace the ones who run a bath and help you in and out of it, but these relationships are real and can matter in difficult times. Given time and intensity enough, some of these occasional meetings turn into friendships – as I have come to know both Marsha and Jack as close friends and as Te Ripowai has come to be Marsha's sister. A friend who needs an airplane ticket to show up can't replace the one who shares every Sunday's walk, but all the same, the friendship carries obligations across distance. As we who met twenty and more years ago grow older, we more often have to work out how to be good distant neighbors and good dispersed friends as we and the people we care about suffer disease and hard times at distances too great for us to be in physical touch. The duration of diseases like Marsha's cancer challenges even the closest dispersed friendship. If good looks or good planning can bring us together for a few days of the months of dealing with cycles of treatment, uncertainty, and fear, that is a mutual gift; but what about all of the days our lives that keep us far apart?

A detached social critic might say that distant neighbors and dispersed friends are a contradiction too far, no more than a rationalization to cover pervasive alienation. But that view would discount what it felt like to some of us to discover ourselves as part of the extended web of support whose edited record you have just finished reading. And that discounting might overlook some small and good efforts to use the electronic tools that come to hand to make ourselves a bit more reliable and decent to those we care for.

So first, some reflection on the nature of the correspondence collected here; then, a sort of inventory of the ways people have been of help from a distance to Marsha and Jack.

The web of support looking from the center out

One way in which the contributors to this correspondence supported Marsha and Jack was by their belonging to a web listed in the address book of Jack's e-mail program. The existence of this web, as a source of occasional messages and as a sort of an audience, was itself a help.

Though we read a collection of e-mail letters, the messages are not disembodied in the way that most messages between participants in an internet chat-room or e-mail list are. Each correspondent also has an in-person relationship with Marsha and Jack - some long and close, some brief, most in-between. Some correspondents know or at least would recognize many of the others in person. A number of people reached out in other ways sometimes with a letter, with a card, with a fax, with a phone call, with a visit, with a gift. Others were fortunate enough to meet Marsha and Jack while they were on the road between treatments and in the months between the two visits with cancer chronicled here.

Throughout the correspondence, Marsha and Jack were at the hub of many spokes. With a few exceptions, like Judith's orchestration of simultaneous songs and visualizations, messages came to them but did not also go to others on their distribution list (in the jargon of the internet, this was not a

Afterword

listserve). E-mail allowed them to pace the flow of reading and responding to individual messages, save messages for re-reading, and take responsibility for composing occasional messages for the whole web of support. This process of composition pro-vided regular occasions to pull together the news, echo some of the individual messages, and share the lessons emerging.

In circumstances that erode the sense of being in control, this was a form of support more controllable than that offered by a ringing telephone or a ringing doorbell. This support may have been much less materially real, but it reinforced Jack and Marsha's control of an important aspect of their lives. Living with cancer didn't mean losing touch with colleagues, and it was possible to stay in touch with many of us on easy terms by saving reading or responding to our e-mails until time and energy seemed right.

In sharing the news about important medical events, Jack managed to convey many concrete details about dealing artfully with the often-bewildering string of events that define contemporary medical treatment from the patient's viewpoint. His accounts prepare those of us who have not yet made the journey through cancer therapy for schedule slips and the horrible routine delays between test and interpreted results. His logs of trips that blend soul-satisfying work with soul satisfying leisure demonstrate the survival value of doing as much of what you love that disease will allow. These guides to the new world of oncology and their intermixed travelogues served the double function of helping Jack make sense of his life at a time when he is often confronted with the inability to do or even predict very much and to turn his personal experience into a source of guidance and even, in the descriptions of travel and visits, into pleasure for his friends.

As the months went by, Marsha made more use of her occasional broadcasts to try out ways to express the lessons she found in her experience. It may not be too much to think that the written informality of e-mail gave Marsha an opportunity to continue to fill the role of teacher, which is so close to the heart of her identity, even when she was physically and emotionally too tired to travel and stand up in front of a group to speak or sit down at the computer to write more structured papers or more disciplined poems. It also allowed her the chance to fulfill her role as one who serves by accepting the risk of publicly speaking out concerning important, but usually avoided, truths.

Members of the smaller telephone and e-mail circle with whom Marsha chose to explore events got a sense of the responsibility Marsha felt for caring for and teaching the larger circle of people on the broadcast list. Many of her messages involved her puzzling about whether she should share a particular experience with the whole web, or seeking advice about whether a particular thought was clear enough for others to understand.

Marsha and Jack discovered that the art of living with cancer includes remembering who you are by doing as many of the things that matter most to you as you can, while overactive and blindly chaotic cells work to dismember you. Writing e-mail to teach their support web by describing and reflecting on what it is like to live the flow of feelings and events around their disease, gave Marsha and Jack an adapted way to do their work that turned into a new way of working. The range of responses from members of the web – some enthusiastic, some reflective – confirmed the meaning in both the content and the role of Marsha and Jack's teaching.

The web of support looking from the edges in

Some people join me in appreciating the grace with which others move quickly and surely toward another's need. These graceful others seem marvellously less self-conscious or less reticent than we are. For us, who resonate with the e-mails that begin, "I'm not very good at this sort of thing, but here goes…", this correspondence includes a wealth of models. Here, then, the lessons one shy person finds in appreciation of his fellow correspondents' contributions.

Presence matters. You don't have to be eloquent or cosmically certain of producing good results to say, "We are with you." "We are thinking of you." "We love you." Of course, many correspondents are eloquent in these fundamental expressions and a few do seem certain that what they have to say will do good. E-mail lets us show up when Marsha and Jack want to read us. It is less intrusive than a phone call or a knock at the door.

Spirit matters. The myriad ways of invoking spirit testifies to the diversity of this web. Correspondents offer straightforward prayers to the God they know loves and watches over them and their friends. They invoke the warrior spirit. They call on the earth and its peoples and its goddesses to uphold Marsha and Jack in their battles. They burn candles. They meditate or enter their silence with the intention of holding Marsha and Jack central in their consciousness. They call a whole tribe to prayer. They call attention to the presence of angels. They cry out to the universe with anger and fear. They send healing light, healing vibrations, healing energies, and love through an ether that lies somewhere further along (or probably outside) the electromagnetic spectrum that carries the pulses of e-mail. They dance. They chant in Tibetan or First Nation's style. They make music. They perform a haka (Maori war dance) to terrify the cancer. They listen to music. They offer up their "prayer equivalents." They hold and warm rose quartz pieces. They share stories and quotes and images that carry spiritual meaning for them. They ritually blow bubbles. They raise the imagination of outrageously diverting acts, like spray painting "Cancer SUCKS!" on Toronto's signature CN

Afterword

Tower. They think good thoughts for and of Marsha and Jack at crucial moments. They send the image of monks of another faith at prayer.

In my faith, there is a tradition of sacramentals, observances not formally reckoned among the sacraments but understood as an outward sign of the effects of grace. From this point of view, it may not be blasphemy to understand some of these e-mails as a sort of second-order sacramental: signs of actions taken as signs of grace.

Offers matter whether they fit the moment's need or not. "Call anytime" and "I'll come when you need me" provide support whether or not the offerers phone rings. So does, "Want some audio-books?"… "No, but thanks."

Responses matter. Requests for a focus of spiritual energy at a particular time are acknowledged. Expressed desire for good mystery books calls forth recommendations and packages. Anxiety that the perception of poor health will result in loss of work returns confirmations of bookings already made and requests for future engagements. Acknowledgements of lessons received and pondered greet Marsha's communication of her sense of what she learns from her visits with cancer.

Confirmations matter. Correspondents acknowledge and validate the flow of feeling that ebbs and flows around the course of disease and treatment. Some of these confirmations come from veterans who have walked a similar path; many are more elemental responses to the fear of pain, uncertainty, death and loss. Some are blunt: "No dying!" Most are more nuanced expressions of what one correspondent calls the sympathy of souls. Other confirmations, in other moods, remind Marsha and Jack of the importance of their role, underlining their contributions as teachers and allies with the expectation that they must find whatever ways possible to continue in those roles. Others simply acknowledge beauty and courage and strength and the paradox of their expression in open statements of fear and confusion. Affirmation of Marsha's destiny is passed along warm from the elders of the Tuhoe people, who have adopted Marsha and Jack: "She knows her task in life is to keep bringing people together – the *whanau* of the world need her."

Different ways to name and understand matter.
Correspondents offer different ways to frame experiences that embody the most fearful aspects of the disease. In Jill's poetastic birthday fashion advice, loss of hair becomes the occasion for adopting a new and sexy look on the way to Marsha's doubling her years and becoming "a cranky, 104 year old, long haired Jew." In Shafik's hands death and pain and misery become inevitable completions whose postponement simply offers the space for continuing important work in service of justice and gratefully acknowledging the gifts of interdependence that allow both him and the people he re-names Thunder and Lightening to sign themselves, "One who has

been caught." In Te Ripowai's Maori – English poetry, Marsha's warrior-spirit mobilizes and allies with the earth's flowers and her dear friend's deep feeling and the model of Tk-niwha against Whiro's monster disciple (Maori mythology) who threatens her destruction with a thrashing body-consuming tail.

In conclusion

The politics of this electronic web of support is worth longer consideration than there is room for here. However, it is these politics that point the way to what must be done as next steps from this book.

Most people lack access to the tools to get some of their supports this way. Some simply lack the technology; illiteracy excludes others. We need to work together to take the next steps in the long journey to universal access to literacy broadly understood as among the tools people need to realize their freedom and dignity.

Many people feel tied to jobs that drain them. They are not nourished, as Jack and Marsha are, by a sense that their work makes an important contribution to the world their children and grandchildren will grow up in. We need to challenge one another to discover our gifts, seek work that develops gifts, and create workplaces that nurture gifts.

Most people don't have ways to earn a living that brings

them into contact with so many and varied distant neighbors or allows the freedom to travel and work hard that Marsha and Jack enjoy. Marsha and Jack are not materially rich, but they have both benefited from well supported public education systems and earned decent wages from hard work in programs that governments have funded as investments in the common good. All of us need to sustain and keep searching for better, more effective ways to use public funds for public good, and we urgently need to push back the narrow-minded, mean-spirited political forces that foster cynicism and selfishness while they feed reckless consumerism.

Many who read this book from across Canada's border must consider the millions for whom Marsha's medical care would be beyond financial reach. We need to find ways to assure all of our fellow citizens of a fair chance at access to decent health care.

In considering the politics of Marsha and Jack's particular cancer, a sort of envy could distract from some of this book's most important messages. It is important to our common well-being not to dwell in envy of Marsha and Jack's computers or their work or their income or their access to medicine or their widely thrown circles of friends and supporters. What matters is to consider the work we need to do together to distribute these privileges far more widely. And it is even more important for us to be actively doing that work, as Marsha and

Afterword

Jack have been throughout their lives.

A lifetime of hard work with and for others can bring the harvest of a web of support so large that 160 of them can be in touch by e-mail. Good fortune or the Great Spirit has left Marsha and Jack more strong and more clear in their work. We all have the option to find our own path to join in this work in our own ways and places and times.

The Sea Venturer Quartet

In July of 1998, we took an incredible nine day scuba trip with Exta Sea Charters Adventure Diving to the Broken Islands of the Barkley Sound region of British Columbia. We had lost too many friends during the past year (1997-1998). Hardial, Shafik, Raniera, Anihaka, Herb, Maria. My heart was full of many feelings. I wrote this quartet on the Sea Venturer – our scuba diving boat that week.

Marsha Forest & Jack Pearpoint

The Sorrow and the Eagle

Tears of joy and of awe jump from my eyes
as the power of the eagle
and the majesty of the landscape
come into view.

This contrasts to the sharp pain in my chest.

I put on my scuba gear.
I fall backwards into the cold Pacific water
which wakens me to life once again.

My body,
exhausted from the sheer physical exertion,
forgets the sorrow for just a few minutes
as I drink in the symphony
of pink rock and waving kelp.

I see the eagle
Flying high over the land
and I weep at last.

Reflection #2

I am awed.
Awed with the sheer beauty of this landscape.
Awed with the sheer beauty of life
and still I feel the raw pain of loss.

Facing life and death, I live more fully,
I feel more intensely.
I listen more. I speak less.
I love more.

Watching too many friends die,
living with my own uncertainty,
knowing in fact
that nothing but the tides are certain,
I often feel vulnerable and scared.

Here in the midst of the Pacific ocean
surrounded by pure beauty
above and below the sea,
I feel a symphony of life surround me.

Today, the green seems greener.
Today, the grief seems deeper.
Today, the joy is quieter.
Today, the ocean is deeper.

Reflection #3

The breeze tosses memories
of loss and love at me.
The truly dead are only those
who are not loved.

In watching death,
in tasting grief and pain,
I am no longer the same.

I see clearly that even in death
the power of love
transcends this finality.

Those who are loved
truly never die.
Their physical being may be gone
but they are here with us
for as long
as we remember.

Reflection #4

This is sure.
The tide will come in.
The tide will go out.
There is even a chart I can read to
tell me this truth.
That's about all I am sure of.

I am loved.
I love.
The rest is fate, chance, and mystery.
All I can do is
get up
face the fear
and live.

July 20, 1998

INCLUSION PRESS INTERNATIONAL
ORDER FORM
24 Thome Crescent
Toronto, ON   Canada M6H 2S5
Tel 416-658-5363 Fax 416-658-5067
E-mail: 74640.1124@compuserve.com

WEB PAGE: http://inclusion.com

Oct. 1998 edition

Classic Videos

With a Little Help From My Friends
Prod: M. Forest & G. Flynn
The basics of creating schools where all kids belong and learn together. Hands on strategies – MAPS & Circles of Friends.

Kids Belong Together
Prod: People First Assoc of Lethbridge, Alta Featuring the late Fr. Patrick Mackan – a celebration of friendship – MAPS in action.

Together We're Better *Video*
Producer: Comforty Media Concepts
Staff Development Kit: a 2 hour video 3-pack of resources with Marsha Forest, Jack Pearpoint and Judith Snow demonstrating MAPS, PATH and CIRCLES. An inspiration.

Miller's MAP *Video*
Prod: Expectations Unltd &Inclusion Press
Children, parents, neighbors and professionals make inclusion happen– team facilitation and graphics in a MAP.

Friends of ...Clubs *Video*
Producers: Oregon Dept. of Education & University of Oregon A beautiful 15 min. story about creating community partnerships. Friends, friends, friends - the spark of life.

Dream Catchers *Video*
Producer: Institute on Disability, NH
New 16 minute video about dreams and circles of friends. Beautiful images, personal stories, images of the future. An inspiration.

Inclusion News
The Center publishes an independent annual newspaper - articles & resources you need . It has raving fans! International flair. Order in volume - $50 for a box of 150. A Conference Must!

Inclusion Exclusion Poster
by Jack Pearpoint
A vibrant eye catching 18" X 24" graphic poster exploring the why behind Inclusion and Exclusion.

Courses for your consideration...